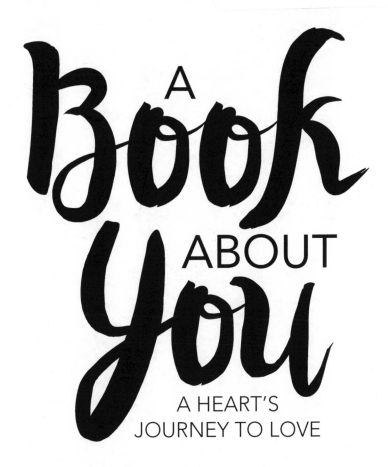

A Book About You

A HEART'S JOURNEY TO LOVE

TONIO

ISBN-13:978-0692678640 (I-Am Love Publications)
ISBN-10:0692678646

*"Love is superfood for the soul.
Consume it in abundance."*

—Tonio

From me to you

It's unbelievable to think we've made it this far. But here we are nonetheless. I honestly couldn't have made this dream come true if it weren't for all of you who believed in me—way before I could believe in myself. Words simply cannot thank you enough for how immensely grateful I am for each and every one of you who pushed and begged for me to publicize this book. For that, I am dedicating this book to you.

Introduction

I can't remember ever wanting to write a book before. I remember writing as a hobby and a way to express myself, as a more comfortable, fulfilling alternative to speaking. I had always written stories and detailed expressions of my innermost feelings and thoughts, but they were always kept in notebooks in the house, which I have misplaced. But, no, I had never dreamed of actually writing a book.

But that began to change at the end of February 2009, when I had a breakup that left me a little lost. I was 21, and was battling with all types of emotions that were real and very new to me. I remember sitting at work one morning in the parking lot where I was a valet supervisor, and beginning to write what is now the poem "Lost a Love" for some strange reason. I posted it on Facebook, not thinking much about it. Almost immediately, friends started to comment on it and to express their heartfelt concerns for me, even though for me this poem was more a reflection—a way to cope with the pain of my loss. But my readers were truly feeling the poem.

This inspired me to write other poems, and before I knew it I was writing more and more, feeling complete with every new poem I finished—and more and more people began to read them. Still, at this point I had no idea what I wanted to do with them. I just wrote. I don't think I was even aware that people wrote poetry books.

It was in 2011 that I first thought of making a book out of the many poems I had written over the past two years. It all began when I woke up one day and said, "A Book About You"—and I've kept this title with me for all these years. For it was an inspired title, inspired by the presence of the powerful word "You" in virtually all of my poems, as an expression of my entity of love—an unknown love without a name or face. However, through my journey of self-discovery and emotional growth, I realized I was my "you"—and we all have a "you": that love we lost, that love we discovered, that special someone we love, that someone we want to love.

Throughout my poems, "you" was meant to be relatable to anyone who would read the book and feel that it was truly about them, feel it as their own, so they would insert themselves, their own experiences, into the narratives of the poems. Which was an even better reason for me to collect my poems in book form—to help people find the "you" in themselves, to relate to their own experiences of pain, to help them realize that "you" are not alone in longing for love.

A series of events, both pleasant and unpleasant, finalized my decision to publish the book. On March 11, 2015, I was a victim of gun violence. Two men—one with a knife, another with a gun—attacked me while I was coming out of my car one night. Watching my whole life flash across my face in the aftermath of the assault left me feeling scared—not necessarily by the threat of death, but by all I had left unsaid and undone. And I was hoping that the ones I loved *knew* I loved them, even though I hadn't said so. This incident also triggered memories of how I wanted to experience real love, even if it was for one moment, before I died—which was the subject of many of the poems I had written so far.

A more benign sign that it was time to publish came from my supervisor, Jaqueline Linton. One day, as we were sitting in her office, she suddenly said, "I know you weren't born to do this job, and we all have bills to pay, but I hope you are going to do something with your writing. You have talent—a gift from God—so don't let it go to waste. He doesn't give this gift to everybody." Her touching remark recalled the many friends, and even people I hadn't met or personally known, who had asked me over Facebook and Instagram if I had a book out and told me it definitely needed to be published, for I had touched their hearts and souls with my poetry. This, combined with the bullet wound scar on my left leg that continues to remind me how fragile life is, propelled me to finally collect my poems into a book and get it out there.

And here it is—*A Book About You*. Yes, it is true to its title—for love is a universal language that expresses a universal human need. For instance, in "34 Kisses," you can feel the love settling in, and you can envision the kisses and how magical the moment was when love finally arrived and took claim of your once fearful heart. And poems like "Airplane Mode" and "Traffic" are only a couple of examples of poems that indicate what love is like today: exciting yet ephemeral, desirable yet deceptive, ideal yet unreal, lost yet worth finding again.

People need to understand that real love is not like what we see in the movies. It is similar, but not exactly the same, for it has many different layers of complexity, contradiction and confusion, some messy and unsettling. But, no matter what, love does not diminish. It merely grows stronger with every battle fought to earn it—or to get away from it.

A Book About You is designed to be read like a journey through love—a journey of highs and lows, moments of happiness and sadness, loss and reconciliation, pain and gain. The book covers my own poetic journey chronologically from 2009 to 2016, and you will notice some of my earlier pieces are longer and more emotionally raw. You can also witness the emotional growth of the writer through those years, as well as the concurrent development of my style of writing. I wanted to keep it that way, so I could remember the innocence of a virgin heart, compared to a heart that has now lived, experienced love, and thereby achieved a higher level of emotional maturity.

You will notice that my poems do not try to rhyme. Any rhyming lines you may see happened out of pure chance, pure coincidence. For, unlike the love of yore expressed in the rigidly structured sonnets of Shakespeare, Keats et al., modern love does not always rhyme, given how unstable, unpredictable, erratic, vulnerable and ever-changing it has become. That is why I am able to take different words and marry them into something beautiful without forcing rhyme or rhythm into them—for love cannot be forced.

Besides, people don't want as much structure today. Our lives are already too structured as they are, and love is not—and should never be, for that would limit its potential to grow, to change, to deepen, even to recede. This also relates to the way writing poetry gives me a freedom to let my mind go where it wants to go, and to go where the heart is, which is always beyond boundaries, barriers, limits…and especially structures.

My poems are therefore an easier, more fluid read than traditionally structured ones, ranging from simple to complex (as an expression of the multifarious characteristics of love), requiring you to think about what they mean and to insert your own situation into them. And they have reached my intended audience very well in this way. Some of my readers initially didn't like poetry, but once they began to read my work, they looked forward to more of it as a means of coping with lost, unrequited or uncertain love, or simply as entertainment.

Some of the poems may not relate to your personal situation—but that's okay. We do not all experience the same hurt or the same love. Like snowflakes, no two love stories are ever alike, and no two phases of one's own love journey are ever the same. Yet, through my poems, I hope to teach every man and woman a universal truth that applies to all love stories and stages: love begins with a choice to listen to the daily moments in life in which a slight feeling of joy turns in to a radiant burst of heart-fluttering sensations. This is the smallest touch, or the first inkling of possibility, that leads you back to love.

And this is how I hope to inspire hope once again in a hopeless heart, to leave my readers with a craving for love, and, most of all, to provide insight into what real love is so they don't settle for that which is familiar, artificial or archaic. For society has changed, and the way we love and date has also changed. Now everything seems to be temporary, and fewer people are courageous enough to save a relationship, save a love. Instead, they move on to another love, and another, and another (hence the high divorce rate and the exploding popularity of online dating and singles groups), often avoiding love altogether in the process.

A Book About You is not just *about* you—it is also *for* you. It is for every broken heart, every crushed spirit, and every heart in love. In this book I invite you to find your story, discover your voice, and embrace every new chapter of your love story as it unfolds. And I promise you that love will arrive willingly. It may take a while, but this book is an opportunity for you to romance yourself in the meantime and prepare for the same extraordinary journey I continue to prepare for, through the very writing of my poetry: love everlasting.

With love,
Tonio

A Book

ABOUT

You

A HEART'S
JOURNEY TO LOVE

Relive your heart's journey...

Honor Love

We've all met that someone we thought to be special,
Perhaps our final destination, even—
In search of love,
Giving freely,
Unexpectedly without measure,
Feeling so alive, so brand new—
But all that quickly got old.
We got hurt.
We got bitter and confused.
We got played.
We got used.
And so we thought, 'Never mind love,'
Forgetting it isn't our fault—
Nor should we feel ashamed, because
Love honors those who honor love back.

Love Out Loud

In the presence of an audience
You loved me.
When it mattered most,
You couldn't.
It was all a façade,
A loud admiration of the surface,
The beauty—
But never the being.
And as I became accustomed,
Ironically, you silenced my desire for reality,
Making of my dreams a play
Scripted and directed by you,
Where love is played out loud
For praise and applause,
And during every intermission,
The charm would disappear
To reveal again the monster, I chose.

Oasis

All around me
The world is quickly becoming a love desert.
Dry conversations,
Misleading personalities,
Camouflaged intentions—
All of which change so suddenly by nightfall,
But not you—
My miracle in the desert,
My oasis of love,
My source of hope where love thrives.

The Rose

Tucked gently on the windshield of your car,
It was a promise of everything unexpected
I had hoped to give
The first time in forever,
Where I wanted to be romantic,
Feeling so emotionally aroused,
Ready to be,
Ready to become
The love, the one.
Instead, something else happened,
And I'm nothing to you.
But I wonder every now and then
What happened to the rose—
What happened to my love?

Caffeine

I was addicted—
No doubt about it.
Something about the way you tasted,
The excitement I got from your aroma,
A feeling of elation.
I loved you
Flying high every time I consumed,
Assuming you were good for me,
Ignoring all your adverse affects,
Not realizing you were a temporary fix
Until you were no more.
Crashing so hard,
Falling deep into a jittery world of solitude
Without caffeine,
Without you.

love will forever remain a mystery,
Despite all the books
With relationship rules
And guide to love.
It so happens
That no love story is ever alike,
Nor will they ever be.
There is no secret formula you can follow
But your heart.

The Art of Love

You and i, a canvas.
And love, the masterpiece.
A collage of sorts
Abstract in nature,
Beautifully painted to begin
Pieces of you, pieces of me—
And it all got so unrecognizably messy,
Difficult to interpret,
But all the more alluring.
I suppose love is this way sometimes.

A Horror Story

You acted so realistically in every scene,
So much that I couldn't tell fact from fiction
Until it ended.
And what I thought to be a romantic fairytale
I now know as nothing but a horror story.

Promises

I suppose I just never cared enough to buy in.
Seems today
Love is just an idea we entertain—
A hobby of sorts
Where fleeting desires inspire words,
And they're just that.
Promises, none of which are kept,
Are made like cheap goods on the assembly line.
It's everyday, it's constant, with no real value.
Sometimes I want to believe
And invest,
But I know too well the fate of those
Who cling to promises of love
As if—
And they wonder why it never lasts.

34 Kisses

It began with a promise from your eyes,
Somehow in the way you looked at me,
Something in the way they saw me,
And I knew it to be real—nothing further from the truth.
Yet—there I was holding back—fearful to disarm,
Afraid you, too, would harm my heart,
Until you took my hand.
Kissing it with intent,
I smiled assuringly,
Welcoming the first of 34 kisses,
All of which became your allies in rescuing my heart.
You see, I had no idea how selfish I'd become,
Imprisoning my heart, feeding it fear, keeping it there,
Meanwhile lying so we still could co-exist.
But no. You were different. You were commanding.
On a mission.
The first was gentle in approach,
Sealing my lips shut,
The second carefully caressed my forehead,
While the third, fourth and fifth were sporadic—and forceful,
Pulling me in further,
Losing track of my heart,
Immersed in a moment where my entire face was loved,
Brought back to life
By every kiss thereafter.
And all I could do
Was count, as if to distract
While you retracted my heart

From that place of infinite darkness and hopelessness.
My eyes would open after 34 kisses, to be exact,
Feeling extraordinarily beautiful in every way.
I smiled to speak,
And you without saying
Knew I no longer was the same.
I'd been saved.

The Lock

Thought you'd come back
Unannounced and uninvited,
Thinking you still had access
Despite everything.
And I don't blame for you thinking so.
After all, it's my fault,
Allowing my love to become customary,
Comedic in how swiftly I'd forget,
Accepting it all for love's sake.
You knew that well—
Especially how to break in and invade my heart,
Taking all of which was valuable to you.
Never-mind my feelings, my needs—
I wasn't someone. I was only something. An object of desire
Attractively packaged.
A beautiful house with open windows and doors,
A magnet for thieves of everything superficial
On a dead end to nowhere.
And here you are once again,
Knocking confidently on a door that's never been closed.
Strange, you thought.
Everything still looked the same on the outside.
Nothing's changed—but something did: the lock.

You and I,
An unexpected and unlikely love story
So original and captivating,
Necessary of a copyright.

It's an unbearable discomfort
Having to pretend to want someone you don't,
Fearful you'll hurt their feelings,
And, worse yet, when they're ideally suited.
But love isn't found on ideals.
Instead, it is found in what is unconventionally
comforting.

No Returns

It was not stolen, nor given.
In fact, you won it.
At the first sight of your smile,
It was awoken,
Then tickled with your pronunciation of my name.
Guards came down,
And suddenly the possibility
To finally live and love
Was imminent.
It had become yours to keep, love and cherish.
I had no problem with you winning,
Because, after all, you played a fair game.
The word 'perfect' began to have meaning,
And so did my life.
With you, it found a safe place and called it home—
A loving home, to say the least.
Unfortunately, unknown forces are impelling.
We take different roads from here on.
Today, we stand at a crossroads
Of uncertainties and differences.
The home we built has crumbled,
Leaving buried in the rubble
Words we once spoke,
And the memories that live on
Haunt us without mercy.
Although our home has collapsed,

I know it could not have found a safer place
Than with you.
So please, if it's not too much to ask,
I would like to have my heart back
Before I take the first step on the new road.
I will not be complete,
But it was and still is
The best part of me.

When You Lose Sight

Once again I can feel it
Torn into pieces inside me,
Tearing up, in and out uncontrollably.
I can hardly see the words I write.
I've lost sight with time,
I've lost sight with tears,
No one is around to hold me as I fall.
I didn't choose to love you.
It happened, and now it hurts,
Crushed to nothing,
And still it lives on.
If I could, I would kill this love,
Undying as it is unforgettable.
My only regret, nothing—
As it is all that came from this.

Where Love Settles

Sometimes I find it incredible
How stupid I am,
How stupid I've been,
Having found all that is worth keeping with you,
And yet I keep searching
For nothing but an ideal.

Sometimes I cry
Knowing I could lose your smile,
Your thoughts of me,
And ultimately my place in your heart.

But you know I'm an idiot,
And so are you—
But we love that about one another.
Our love is unpredictable and reckless,
Fighting just because
Even the angry side has its rare beauty
In which we bask.

Acceptance became our virtue,
Love became our ally.
We became soulmates.

We laugh because we can be incredibly silly at times.
No matter the setting,
We make others crave this kind of love
That never hides from the truth,
Never settles anywhere but here
In my heart. In yours. Forever.

Enough

Couldn't think of a way to say, 'Enough.'
Love itself isn't routine.
It's always exciting, always evolving,
And yet there I was—stuck,
Tear after tear, night after night,
Holding on to nothing but a false hope
That someday soon, things will change—
You will change.

But I was wrong, so wrong.
You couldn't care less for the loss of my smile,
Loss of sight, loss of sense, loss of light.
I was nothing but a convenience,
An ego booster, a loser.
But it's fine—now it's time.

Tired of trying when I can just be.
Tired of you, always finding fault,
Pointing a finger in every direction but your own,
Tired of forcing a smile, even when it hurts.

But how do you say goodbye
When you're too involved?
Eternity became the long painful days
Of the constant vowing to be strong,
To move on without cares.

But how do you move on
When you've left everything behind
Where and with whom it shouldn't be?
No one is immune to a heartbreak—this is a fact.
Be you the most beautiful, be you the most extraordinary,
It will happen when you give carelessly.
I wish I knew how to feel so I could feel something.
That's what this love has done to me.
This love is not worth another tear,
Not a single more tear.

I've begun learning to have other thoughts—
Happy ones of gain, not loss—because, after all,
True love never takes away from.
It adds to each and every single aspect of life.
My life. Our life. We had neither together.
Goodbye.

inked

I made the mistake of writing with a pen,
Confident in our story,
In what we had compiled,
Believing it would never end,
Thinking I'd never have to erase,
Wanting it all to remain
Written forever.
But you'd tear up the pages,
Many of which I dedicated my life to creating,
Forgetting you never wanted to be a character in my book,
Let alone the protagonist.
I was so busy loving you,
Missing the errors,
Never minding your mistakes,
Too involved to edit what read so beautifully.
And love is that way sometimes—unedited—
But it always makes sense.
Not this story though. Not our story.
Rightfully so, I'm ashamed,
Wishing I could erase history,
But I can't.
Meanwhile, I frantically scribble over these pages
In efforts to cover up the bruises inked in my heart,
Attempting to hide the words that still haunt—
But I can't.

my heart,
Captured into slavery,
Punished and abused
Simply for loving
A master of disguise.

Heart in Captivity

Before you,
I thought I knew
Everything there was,
Everything love is.
But you'd kiss me once,
Look twice,
And that was it.
Suddenly I wanted,
Eager to explore this enchanting desire to belong,
Basked in the glow of your smile,
Danced to the sound of your voice
As it sang my heart into captivity.

Delete

Thinking I could,
And so I should,
I tried
Deleting
Messages, images, and videos of you, of us.
Thinking it easy,
Thinking it over,
But I would wonder,
Holding on,
Remembering every saved memory,
Every captured moment,
Suddenly teary,
Suddenly confused,
Angrily blaming myself,
Thinking perhaps if—
But this is the reality.

I must delete what torments,
What pains,
What lingers,
While yearning for what is no longer.
Becoming harder—weaker—
Impossible to let go.

Mustering courage,
Fighting off thoughts which want to live on,

Hindering my heart,
I chose to delete a love saved—
Only to find it again and again
Restored in my memories of you.

Antagonistic Love

Perhaps it's the echo of your voice
Still lingering in the air
Or the silence of my heart in mourning
That brings me down to my knees.
And I'm here, on unfamiliar grounds,
Attempting to bury memories
Much too painful
In the wake of your betrayal.
And now my fight for survival
Against an antagonistic love
As undying as it is unsettling.

Airplane Mode

Taking off was exciting—
I could feel my heart flying,
Fueled by promises of newness.
You and I,
Soaring above the sky
To a new high,
Leaving behind the oldness
Of our troubling past
And failed attempts,
Our fleeing hearts finally buckled,
Awaiting love's arrival.
This was it. You insisted I'm your answered prayer,
The dream in human form. Here. Now.
I wanted to believe for a change
Perhaps this could be, even though—
So I went along for a ride,
Neither one of us prepared.
Just as quickly, turbulence
Would release all your baggage,
Testing my will,
Descending my heart from the clouds,
Because, truth is, you weren't available.
We weren't on the same flight.
You weren't whole.
You had a dream—
Not your heart.
Everything I wanted you couldn't give.
Not then. Not now. Not ever.

Your heart still belonged to a turbulent past,
An undying love,
And I was to wait patiently on airplane mode,
Hoping for a signal,
A secure connection
Where the past won't interfere.
But I feared my heart landing
In the hands of someone unattainable.

A Moment in Time

A single smile and an exquisite taste remained—
An unexpected pleasure, a newfound passion.
After it happened,
The smell of hope lingered in the air for hours
While inside we danced with excitement
At the thought of new possibilities.
In a moment's time, love would touch me one true time,
Redefining life as I knew it to be before you.
Whispering your invitation,
Slowly I crawled my way into your arms
Where the touch of magic was immanent.
Afraid to get so close, I thought to run—I thought to hide.
In the end I thought a million things,
But none as powerful as the sound of your voice,
The strength of your stare
Entrapping every part of me
And yet feeling so free.

Alive and well,
I could smell love.
I could hear the amazing sounds from within and again,
The whispers from the mouth I would kiss—
Tantalizing with a fiery passion
That came from the warmth of your hands as they touched my
skin.
Face to face, eye to eye, there we were,
Exploring the contours of each other's face,
The extent of a great smile.

Over and over our fingers ran gently across and around,
Finding familiarity in a dream come true.
I could feel the trembling of my hands
As they caressed your face for the first time,
My nose against the softness of your lips
So delicately shaped, colored in red—perfect red—perfect fit—
The sound of your breathing, powerful,
And yet pleasing to my ear,
Where comfort and peace became a blanket of love—
A small peck, here and there savoring every moment,
Healing all wounds, starting anew.

Late Night Craving

I guess I thought I'd miss you a little while longer and then forget,
But it didn't turn out that way.
It's been many months,
And I still crave the sound of your heartbeat,
Wishing I'd wake up to the smell of your hair.
But instead all I smell is dead air
In a bed so uncomfortable without your warmth,
Tossing and turning,
Wondering if you still think of me,
If you still care.

I keep going back,
Wanting to look
Just one more time,
And then another,
Trembling with excitement,
Gasping for air,
Fearful I might fall
Watching you smile,
Praying it is real,
Hoping you'll be something more
Than just a dream.

5 Years

I'm trying to hide,
Holding my head up high
While failing to hold back memories
Once beautiful, now painful—
Digging to bury this hurt eating me up,
Creating noise any way I can
To silence the muffled screams of my aching heart,
Mourning the loss of the unworthy
Who abused and misused
A beautiful heart
Barely recognizable,
Faintly beating.
I'm ashamed.
5 years—
Such a long time.
And now it's all a blur,
Unable to see with eyes filled with tears,
Wondering what I did with my life all these years.

Loving intently and effortlessly,
Adding to what I thought was concrete and worth building,
But it would all crumble in a moment's time,
Ending in utter silence.
No apologies. No goodbye.

TONIO

Because I wasn't enough, I suppose.
And to think I gave 5 years of trust and loyalty,
Some of my best—
And yet it meant absolutely nothing
As I watch my love sink deeper and deeper into nothingness.

Cold War

It is indeed the loneliest hour.
Having gone to war without weapons,
Knowing I'd be losing the only love I've known,
Battling with difficult words, yet unknown,
Never before dreamt—
But we weren't meant,
So I assumed it was time
To end and let go
Once and for all,
Enduring the dreadful pain of losing,
Hoping in the end I'll gain something—anything.
But someone like you,
Incapable of fighting back—
And you couldn't—not when
You never had my back.
So I understood by your silence
Nothing ever really mattered—
Not I, not my love, not my sacrifices.
Hence you couldn't hear
The echoes of my pleading, bleeding heart,
Wishing you'd say something, anything to end this war.
But no. Instead you said nothing.
I would in turn, with much dismay,
Dismiss my heart's intent
And speak what few words I could remember,

Feeling so anxious, so disgusted
That it was, in fact, time I end
This cold war between us.

Cry

Enslaved into captivity.
Held back.
Threatened to silence.
Hiding the truth.
Hiding the story.
Millions of words,
Soldiers of love fighting for freedom
Wanting to be spoken,
Wanting to be heard,
While I denied them the liberty
To roll off my tongue
And free my soul.
I didn't want to depend
Nor ever bend.
I'm the ruler of this universe,
Governed by silence.
But I could feel them choking me,
Inciting war within,
Evoking emotions I'd long forgotten.
And now I'm beginning
To cower in fear,
Ready to surrender
To this rainstorm of tears
Hurrying down my cheeks—
A loud cry, and then freedom.

The Dream

That day
That was yesterday
Back when I thought,
Faithfully believing it so,
Swearing it true,
Wanting nothing more,
I loved and adored,
Even when it hurt
Coming back for more—
Quite the norm
That was yesterday.
Forgiving for that is love.
Allowing for that was the abuse.
You and more you—
All about you,
All I could see
And I—I no longer.
Lost.
Hidden.
Existing so beneath something other than love.
Muted to the point of utter silence
Until today, when I had a dream
Inspiring a hopeful smile in my heart,

And right then
I believed once again
In a tomorrow more promising
Where I live on top of love
Loudly embracing,
Purposefully romancing,
Unmistakably in love.

nothing

A feeling, perhaps
Meant to have no significance,
And yet it troubles my spirit,
Wandering in nothingness,
Wondering in infinite silence,
Trapped in a cycle of impossible thoughts,
Feeling absolutely nothing.
Escaping is just an idea
Much too impossible to execute
While feelings are numb
And emotions have run far and away.
You—a once-upon-a time-fairytale,
A once-in-a-lifetime love—or so I thought,
Now a distant memory
Neither here nor there,
Reduced to nothing
Due to deceit,
Acknowledging was painful,
Accepting was shameful.
My heart, now
Thoughtfully fearful,
Watchfully cautious.
Whatever love we had

Now replaced by indifference,
Not anger, and so
I do not lament,
I do not regret.
I am, however,
Knowledgeably sane enough
To conquer the nothingness and survive,
For in love there are no victims.

i enjoy the silence in which we sometimes exist
With and without words, and yet we understand
What is and yet to be—
You, me—us. An equation of love.

When You Didn't

Took a while to accept
Losing a war
Between love and hate,
Attempting to hide the love,
Failing every time
With the slightest sound of your voice,
Smiling uncontrollably
Simply because you're near,
Mustering a false sense of courage
In order to ignore,
In order to survive,
Wanting to hate all the parts of you I loved,
Finding impossibility with every try.
So I'd cry in silence,
Hoping for a chance at freedom.
But I loved you even more when it hurt.
I loved you even more when you didn't.

Love:

Sometimes it makes absolutely no sense,
But that's the ineffable beauty of it.
However unfamiliar the feelings,
And yet we maintain a profound curiosity
To know and understand all that is this person.

Pride

Long before you came along,
I became good friends with Pride.
He offered excellent protection—
Safety and security came standard.
Finally a friend
Who understood me and always looked out for me.
Together we conquered many hearts,
Only to then break frivolously.
After all, it was always self
Before anyone else.
We were perfect together,
Programmed to quickly dismiss and forget,
Never to look back
And never to wonder.
Never had I shed a single tear,
For I dominated all emotions—
If there were ever any.
Many times I have heard of Love
And how magnificent it is.
Needless to say,
I have always reserved my thoughts and opinions
On the 'enemy'—as Pride liked to call it.
Love, as he put it, was false—
A mere notion of the weak who lack self-control.
Pathetic are those who dare believe or speak of it.
As in our relationship, it was prohibited.

Then, Love decided to pay us a visit.
I remember the day when for the first time I saw you.
And you saw me.
With pride by my side
I could not show excitement.
I could not look.
Somehow you knew
I had been living with the enemy—
He who kept us apart,
Oh, for so long,
As the antagonist of any love story,
He fought and conspired
To destroy Love, to destroy us.
The more I pulled and pushed,
The harder you pulled and pushed
Until you were in,
Showing me a new world, a new friend.
I slowly pulled away from pride,
And it turned out that Pride was the enemy, the weak—
Not you, not Love.
To think all these years fearing and avoiding Love,
Who only wanted peace in my heart, pathetic me.
Soon after, Pride vanished,
And you became my good friend.
My love.

You

You are my love,
Without a face,
Without a name,
And yet I love you.
You are certainty among ambiguity.
You are the unfamiliar feelings I get
Every time we meet.
Ridiculous as it may sound,
This is very true.
You are love in its purest form—
One that lasts
When everything else is gone.
You are faith restored.

Beyond hope, you are a pulling force,
A guiding light in a once-dark soul.
You are life before I was living—
And living I did, when you showed me the way.

If there is anything I am sure of in life, it is you.

You are strength beyond the physical,
And, while fighting time and adversaries,
We conquered love.

You are every step I never took.
Rising above all, you managed to take

That which I could never give,
And in return we made a fair exchange.

You are the keeper of my now vivacious heart,
And, with his definite approval, there will never be another.
You are the peace of mind and the security no money can buy.
You fill my thoughts with purity and beauty that is you.

Before you, I never entered the world of love where all is bright.
You are my beautiful universe that is infinite.
You are my life.

i believe you exist,
Perhaps somewhere
Not far from my imagination.
You, too, are awaiting our moment.

A Night to Remember

It all happened so fast.
You, me—together at last—
And then it all ended just as fast.
But I remember you, me and the moon—
Full and bright,
And the only light
On the night we first met.
Standing beside me was the dream I had crushed
And the hope I had drowned,
Alive and full of life, smiling at me
Who had forgotten how to smile
In your eyes, was the vision I had lost.
Suddenly I was everything by your side,
Fearful, but hopeful—
I sat watching your every gesture,
And then I felt the warmth of your hand against mine,
And, for the first time, I knew comfort.
Your voice became the new genre of music I discovered
And the joyful noise within the confines of my soul.
In the cage, a thunderous heartbeat from he
Who had finally awoken to the sound of love,
Ready to give, ready to receive.
Every passing moment meant more than the one before,
Unlocking every door ever locked.
Fantasy or reality, I cared not to move away from your glow,
Wanting every detail of what makes you.

Again I watched in amazement your glistening eyes
As they spoke to me while your voice sang
With magic floating in the air, unfamiliar feelings,
And the desire to hold and keep soon conquered.
Our bodies then held on together as time stopped,
And we knew this was not just another night.
Despite the many goodbyes, we lingered,
Knowing not that this would be the last—
And with the moon as our only witness,
On this, a night to remember,
I remembered the promises between our hearts
To one day beat as one.

Your Kind of Love

You said you loved me, you thought of me and you needed me.
Then someone else would come along, and just as quickly
You'd notice them and forget you loved me
Because now you thought of them and needed them just the same—
While I watched.
And knowing how I cared and how much I loved you,
You began to toil with my emotions,
Hanging on your every word,
Every promise of love never felt.
Ever given, I remained by your side,
Living in a picture of a perfect relationship you painted
Where the colors washed off every night
When my tears attempted to set me free.
Somehow in the morning, you always noticed,
Because true happiness can't be faked,
And my smile, which had always been sincere, had left my face.
Nevertheless, my sadness wouldn't change your love.
Entrapped in this new kind of love—your love—
I began to assimilate and accept that it was the only love.
And again, deeper and deeper I got buried in lies,
And again, I showed you my love.
Some nights the tears would run out as I wish I could,
But there was no escape for a prisoner of love
Drowning in a tear-pool
Of regret, despair, and hunger for love—
Your kind of love: only told, never shown.

Every night you slept beside me ever so soundly
To the echoes of my weeping heart
As I prayed and hoped someone, anyone, would notice
And make it stop, but no one did. Not a single soul.
With your eyes you looked, but never saw me—
Though you knew I could, and I gave you everything
No one else would or did.
Again, you promised a change so that I would stay.
And I stayed.
Overflowing with hope and a renewed promise of your love,
I began to give more of my love,
Hoping it would cure your blindness
And return to me the love I had always dreamed
But never felt by your side.
And once again, knowing you had me,
You forgot me—for the last time.
You said you loved me, you thought of me and you needed me—
But you never saw me.
And while you forgot me,
I remembered myself.
And as the story went, you began painting the same picture.
Only this time, the colors faded—
And not because of my tears,
But because I no longer saw you underneath it all.
Your cries, I could not hear them,
As I was now deaf.
And so I left,
Because your kind of love is not my kind.

Cancerous Love

Somehow it invaded my body,
Started growing
Bigger and uncontrollably
Inside my heart,
Spreading to the very core of me—
This cancerous love,
A dangerous kind of love
Difficult to remove
Where a victim is claimed
By a villain of love
Self-absorbed,
Incapable of caring
A cheat, rather.
But I'm a fighter,
And I'm tougher,
I keep saying,
But the truth—
The truth is, I still yearn to belong,
Though in excruciating pain,
I'll run back to you,
Having a million things to say—
Funny moments I want to share—
Untold stories of my days passed—
Every song, every moment now a constant reminder
Of you who has pained me deeply,
Betraying all of my trust, all of my love,

And still I love.
'I will survive,
I will be free,'
I keep saying,
But this love is a disease.
And I'm on a mission for remission to eradicate
What is no longer healthy,
Consuming my mind,
Damaging my soul,
Destroying my spirit.

Traffic

We were moving fast,
Changing lanes without signaling.
I was following,
Thinking you wanted me close.
It was fun pursuing,
Not knowing you had no intent on stopping,
I wasn't aware—until we collided.
Your heart was heavily congested,
Confused by all the noise,
All the lovers and promises,
None of which bring you joy.
But you love it—even if for a moment.
It's something to fuel your ego to nowhere,
Stuck in traffic,
And I don't care—
Because I'm exiting soon.

Tomorrow is so far away.
Every moment without you is eternity.
It's crazy to say, but I can't be without you.
Loving you is living.
Sometimes even when you're near, I miss you.
It's a beautiful feeling, knowing we belong,
And I can't imagine a better love.

The Truth in Your Eyes

i knew.

Long before I had proof,
I just knew.
Despite your plea,
It was time I flee.
Whatever your reasons were,
The fact is, you failed me anyway,
Going outside our home
And breaking all our promises.
The thing is, while you said one thing,
Your lips told me a different story.
And your eyes, they evaded my staring,
Fearful I'd catch the lie—
And I did.
For they no longer looked at me
With the same intensity,
Lacking sincerity,
No longer holding the same visions of us.

Just *yesterday*
It was all music to my ears.
And now, a discordant sound
Of uncertainty,
Playing nonstop
All the things you said,
All the lies you told.
And I'm too old
For ambiguity.

Unrequited Love

In my dreams I live
What is perhaps the greatest love story,
But never actualized,
Never realized.
So great I still smile
With every thought
In reality.
I wonder if all this time
You saved me, or I saved you?
Perhaps we'll never know,
But I'm OK,
Although I still feel in love
Still involuntarily yours.
I wonder why—when it seems you're not ready
Or quite frankly uninterested,
So I relive again and again
A similar yet very familiar story
Like all the times before this,
Going around and around,
Questioning and wondering—
A never-ending confusion
More unsaid then said
With each familiar story,
Leaving my fire of desire

Burning low,
Burning out—
Slowly but surely, I hope
Will kill an undying love,
Killing me
While loving you.

Untitled Love

Perfection isn't a reality.
Perfection isn't a thing.
It's a feeling—and you taught me that.
Yes, I noticed your beautiful face,
Your undeniably attractive body,
Exciting parts of me I didn't know could be roused.
Like yourself, I was used to a certain kind of treatment,
Sometimes spoiled, sometimes insufferable,
Tall and proud, my stance
Dismissing futility,
Ignoring stupidity,
Acknowledging this idea of love
But deeming it yonder
Typical behavior of I who met you,
Only to then rediscover life.
What little control I believed to have had!
You took that control,
Asking the daring questions no one else would,
Leaving nothing unsaid.
My mind learned to speak—
My thoughts, suddenly meaningful.
What I didn't see, now I saw,
All because you challenged everything I set forth.
Enough wasn't enough—not when it comes to love.
My pride, you replaced with humility.
My heart, you accepted willfully
Along with everything else, good and bad.
But, despite my fighting, you always fought harder,

Only to introduce the feeling of perfection
In this what we have—
Where I am me, and you are love.

Heart Song

Gently on my chest
You lay your head.
Suddenly the music starts,
And I could feel you smile.
Overcome with joy,
You lay there in peace,
Listening to every word
From my heart to you.
He who could never lie
Would tell you, in a song, words I could not.
In every verse, a new revelation, a greater love,
Pure sounds of joyfulness,
Echoes of a wild loving beast
Ready to be tamed
By only one thing: your love.
An unrehearsed song of love
For your ears, for your heart,
Promises of never-ending love,
Promises to always keep
Even when we fail to see, and
Strength to hold us when weakness invades.
With every running second the music intensifies,
As does your touch, and then silence.
My heart skips a beat
While over your head—
I rest in peace.

The pain that is, missing a part of your life,
A part of your heart
Having given to be taken for granted,
Bounced around battlefields
Filled with tears from all the years,
Every painful moment
Now mudding the ground I walk,
Carefully watching every step,
Hoping to save a memory—
Something, anything,
Even though it hurts
While you fight me off,
No longer needing my love.

One Way

I'm not sure why I drove down that way.
It had always been a one-way,
But I had hoped I could drive back
And things would be different.
Perhaps you'd see me differently—
But no.
Nothing was ever the same, except it hurt more,
Realizing I still love you unrequited.

Play

i have been called beautiful a million times,
And I have cried just as much every time,
Because beauty is all they see—
While hiding behind enemy lines,
Lies the everlasting beauty.
Forsaken tales of love,
Untold stories of life's trials and mishaps
Along with dreams of you,
All stored away, never to be seen, never touched.
In this world where beauty reigns supreme,
Love has little to no chance of living if it isn't real.
Dreams of love, and the desire to love
All get lost behind what lies on the surface—
And this, the norm of the game, so I learned to play,
Becoming whomever, whenever.
Losing is easy, so winning is everything.
Artificiality makes you and then becomes you.
I have lived a thousand lives,
Told a million lies,
And yet no one has cared enough
To look for the truth.
No one has cared enough
To uncover all that is buried
Under what little beauty they see.
And so I have conformed.
I have forgotten how to be and who to be.

In the mirror, I have seen a million different faces,
All of which have looked back at me indifferently,
As strangers do.
With every encounter
A different face
And a different lie—
After all, no one knew, no one cared.
I played every time,
Knowing I would win
Without actually winning,
Because in the end
I could never find you.
It was an easy game
Where the rules were simple:
Pretend, and, of course, show face,
And make sure it is always pretty enough,
Or you won't stand a chance.
I played and played, never getting played,
But always lost somehow—
Or at least that's the feeling I had,
Because after every game I cried.
Silent tears of years forgotten,
Years gone, and still no you.

Lost a Love

I lost a love,
And it's like nothing I've ever felt before.
My heart cries.
I can't hold back the tears that come
Every time my memories decide to torture me.
The constant reminder of the loss
Is enough to drive me insane.
In faces I once saw beauty.
I see them no more.
Everywhere I turn,
There is no light,
Happiness or hope.
I eat and eat to fill in the empty spaces inside,
Only to find that it was all in vain.
I stand all alone in the bathroom mirror,
Staring at a figure
That has been known to represent me
And yet is lifeless.
It has lost its spirit and soul.
As I stand there, I know it is another day
In which I will have to face the world again,
All alone and powerless.
Everything becomes uncertain.
I lost a love, and I'm lost.

Hate Love

Starting to hate love.
Everything about it—
The idea, the word, the meaning—
It's become much of nothing
When nothingness is all we feel
Once it hurts, once it ends.
It no longer is sacrifice,
Nor is it marriage—
Instead, sex, business, and appearance.
It's unclear what love is
When lust is more prevalent,
When independence is arrogance.
We want what we want
When we want it, and
Compromise isn't an option,
Not in this world,
Not in this lifetime,
Give or take someone will always be selfish.
Selflessness is now a mere concept.
Uncertainty is now the future,
Like dreams and broken promises, now the norm.
The truth is hard to find
When we all know how to bury well.
Fear no longer is the enemy of love—we are.
No one is strong enough
To break down barriers and walls.

No one is patient enough
To build concrete relationships, and thus
Hope lives on a lie—
Love lives somewhere in the hearts of dreamers,
But—
Love is what love was—to those who still believe.
I don't.

Pictures of You

I know you are real,
But sometimes I find myself
Looking at pictures of you
In disbelief.
I've scrutinized,
Zoomed in and out,
Attempting to find a flaw
Where it seems impossible.
I know you're not perfect,
But it sure feels that way
Every time we talk,
Every time we message back and forth.
And I need not say more
When we let our hearts speak languages
Not yet known,
Not yet explained.
See, all it took was one moment,
One night for it to last a lifetime—
And, regardless of time and distance,
We remain connected, enchanted, intrigued.
I still can't quite find all the words to describe
What it feels like every time I receive
A new picture of you.
But I love them, I love you,
And all the times you've made me smile,
All the times you've lifted me up and given me hope.

I'm holding on stronger than ever—closer than ever—
Knowing we will continue living
A story we couldn't write better,
Waking and walking every day with each other
With a blessing that it is having,
This, what we call 'us.'
This, what we call love.

Sweet Surrender

Unhappy is the state in which I live,
Insanely in love
With, and at the same time without,
Abusing and torturing every part of me,
Losing every battle against love,
Every battle against you
Whom I love—
Whom I know is love.
There isn't a second of every minute
Where my mind isn't infiltrated
By a thought of you—
However simple it may be,
Still a beautiful thought.

Truth is, I don't know if you know
How I feel, how I hurt in your absence,
How high I soar in your presence,
Or how far I would go for your love.

Some days I hate you for stupid,
For being just as scared as I am,
But it all changes with a single word
And every sight of you.
But how could I blame you when I, too, fear
Perhaps much more than you
When all of this is new and unfamiliar?

I'm left incomplete every time we part,
Every time we greet as friends,
And every time we shy away—
When I have much to say, much to give.

I can feel when you're looking at me,
But I'm too frightened to look back,
And when I do I catch you smiling at me,
I know why, I feel why, but you won't say why,
While I would die to kiss your smile.

Though I act strong,
I wish you knew how weak I feel
Every time you touch,
Every time you are near.

I have prayed a million times
For strength and clarity,
And yet I get weaker
And even more confused,
More involved, more in love.
I can't escape, I can't dismiss,
Because with every attempt,
I see your name in the strangest of places.
Baffled, I surrender yet again.

Artificial Heart

Functional as it was destructive,
Unaware and unassuming,
And yet you assured its authenticity,
Promised a million times over
That it is good.
Carelessly saying,
Freely playing a game of words,
Pretending it was you—when not.
Instead, I found the script in which you borrowed from,
Hoping you'd get in return a significant investment in me.
Every word, every action, every promise
You were taught to repeat long enough
Till someone believes,
Till someone falls.
I didn't.
I couldn't.
So you questioned,
Asked of me,
Made of me less than—
With words of disgrace,
Resenting my lack of love—thereof
And even then—I smiled politely,
Thanking you for such kind words,
Never mentioning the disrespect.
The audacity to give me an artificial heart,
But here is mine.

I never saw the fire burn in your eyes
Nor glisten in my presence,
A common knowledge between true lovers
That wasn't us. I never could feel your kisses,
Let alone embark on journeys.
Every word was simply that:
A word—never understood, never meaningful,
And, although carefully chosen,
Lacked conviction, required honesty—I knew that.
Convenience turned you on, lies guided you,
And appearances motivated you,
But I knew better than to settle.

Reserved

He exists so—
When there was doubt,
You showed me the moment you smiled.
The moment you spoke, he awoke,
Took a look at you,
Who had only been a dream until now.

This was no mistake.
And yet I continue to dream.
You've been away now for quite some time,
And yet he refuses to forget, let alone let go.
I've tried convincing every way I can,
Steering the eye in another direction,
Seeking hope in others,
Finding only falsity.

Sometimes I don't and can't understand why
You aren't here or I there,
Even though I can go
To that place I know is home.
But that day will come,
I know.

It happens with every photo of you,
Every word of every message—

I fall deeper and harder every time,
Gasping for air,
Choking on a million words,
Afraid to look again
For fear he will attack.

I've found my greatest inspiration and strength in you
And all you represent to me.
Voicemails and messages sometimes I wait
Till I find a quiet space
Like that which bears your name,
Hidden from all who hope to claim it—
Unavailable, untouchable, unattainable.

I didn't always know what I want,
Not in life, not in love.
But I know you, I want you.
My feelings, my endless hope for us,
My dreams, your dreams,
They aren't going anywhere.
The very best part of me you have reserved,
And he waits for your return.

In the Face of Love

All it took was one look,
And suddenly a face wasn't just a face anymore.
Behind your smile was an invitation—
Behind your eyes, visions of us.
And though seeing you for the very first time,
Your every essence felt familiar.
Nothing was strange; nothing was new.
I knew someday soon I'd kiss your smile,
I'd kiss your face, that face of love—my face of hope.
Once again I began to dream,
And I could see 'us'—
It was possible—it is possible.
I wanted more than a relationship—
A life, with you,
With mine and yours,
The good and bad parts of you,
I wanted it all.
Assured, the moment you first said hello,
I began to give of me,
And your first compliments touched my once-cold heart,
Desiring from then on only compliments from you,
No one else.

And then we met, and—
All it took was one kiss,
And suddenly I am alive,
I am well,
Understanding life, understanding love,
Powerful as the beat of our hearts
The moment we first touched,
Beautiful as the pronunciations
Of our names together,
Inexplicably enchanting—
Undeniably a miracle of love.

Crave

It comes and goes
Unexpectedly,
Sometimes wanted, sometimes not.
Each time it creates a different taste,
Sometimes bitter, sometimes sweet.
I love it, and then I don't.
I want it, and then I don't.
I could, but I refuse
To allow, to accept
Anything that isn't everything.
I've seen, I've heard, I've tasted,
And I'm not interested.
I could smell the lies,
The eagerness to have what is beautiful
And visually appetizing,
Simply because so—
But I've learned to ignore
The compliments filled with lust—
I must, in honor of love.
Days when the skies are gray
I find it harder to disengage,
Harder to satisfy this craving for love
That infiltrates every part of me
Without reason, without mercy,
Towing my hungry heart yet again
To that familiar state of loneliness

Where I cower and weep,
Engendering feelings of doubt and confusion.
But then I remember why I wait:
I imagine your smile as it will answer every question,
Your touch as it will heal and seal,
Your spirit as it embodies the true love I crave.

Love Ghost

Lately, you've been visiting more than usual—
Flipping back to the pages of a closed chapter
Of a love story once lived.
Like in the first chapter, you come uninvited.
Without a knock or warning,
You infiltrate my mind
And then my soul,
As they are all I have left.
The traitor, who was once my guide and link to Love,
Chose to remain with you
And not me, who protected him.

Of him I wish not to speak, as he betrayed me.
We were not supposed to settle anywhere for too long.
The rule was always clear and simple:
One foot in and one foot out
In case we ever had to run.
I needed to run, and so I did,
Knowing it would kill you.

Now a fugitive of Love, I run but cannot hide,
Because you haunt me with memories and thoughts of you.
In dreams, you take me back to that familiar place
Where for the first time we saw each other and smiled,
Knowing that we'd wake up every time from then on,
And the sun would always shine even when it rained,
Because in each other we found Love—
Love which I couldn't and didn't want to accept,

For fear ruled me.

Just yesterday, as I lay in bed,
You came to me again, whispering words we once shared.
Over and over, I could hear the broken promises,
The many 'I love yous,'
Your laughter and your pronunciation of my name—
All of it tormenting me.
Then the images of us would play over and over in my head,
Only there was no stop button.
In my attempts to escape you,
I thought the television would help—
Except it didn't, it couldn't.
All I could hear was your voice, our laughter,
And how much we loved each other—
Memories so real they paralyzed me in bed.
This time, I could not run
But could see, hear and feel all.

Seeing now what I couldn't see before
Were the many nights you stayed up guiding my sleep,
Tiptoeing your fingers over my face
And then gently kissing my lips.
Here, I remembered there was nothing we wanted more
Than to be with one another, doing absolutely nothing—
And yet it still meant absolutely everything.

You then reminded me of my favorite pastime—
Examining your face inch by inch
And then gazing deep into your eyes
Only to see my reflection, because you saw me.
Beyond my thinking, I relived the moments
When I couldn't leave your side without a kiss.
And sometimes when I would forget,
I would blow you one from across the room,
Where you never failed to catch.

TONIO

Buried deep within the confines of my soul
Was my most treasured memory
Of how your eyes smiled brilliantly
Every time you saw me.

When I thought the torture was over,
You then sprayed the sweet scent of love—
A familiar powerful scent, taking me back
To the night we first made love.
Watching closely the fashion in which we held one another
I knew then I had made the greatest mistake of my life.
I abandoned my heart, the best part of me, and worst of all—
I killed you in the most senseless of ways with my goodbye.

Love in Silence

Entrapped in a dangerous love affair
Alone, with my thoughts and feelings I live,
Harboring a million words, a million gestures,
Countless moments, imagining us as if—when not.
My heart you have—and yet you do not know,
For in your presence I cannot speak of my heart's desire.
And this, the time when I feel most beautiful, most alive,
I know not how to give when I've never given
Or how to break down walls I've built so high,
So strong when I'm so weak—
Therefore my love you cannot see.
In silence, torture is routine
In the battles of questions with no answers:
How do I begin to tell you that I know no safer place
Than beside you—when I know not how you feel?
How do I begin to explain that you have become my world,
An option found nowhere else, when I know not how you feel?
So many ifs and maybes that know nothing but doubt,
And yet they feed it to my brain
While my heart refuses to consume such toxins
Because he knows best.
Meanwhile, I'm running, and yet I get nowhere,
Because you are my final destination,
And so around and around I run,
And every road I take leads back to you—
And yet I cannot confess so that you know.

In every waking moment, thoughts of you fill my mind
Just as beautiful as they are crazy.
When the night comes, my eyes remain closed
While my heart is wide open,
Hoping you'd visit in a dream.
But in silence my heart loves,
While in darkness I live without your love.

Being with you
It is more than a state of being—
Something inexplicably extraordinary,
Existing in moments far beyond what dreams are made of
Where I find, all of which I never thought could be
Blissfully enveloped by infinite love.

Remnants of You

It was supposed to be a step forward,
A chance at a new beginning.
But there's no help but noticing that things are different—
They will always be.
No matter who, no matter where,
There is no you—just an empty world.
Different hopefuls knocking with no answer come and go.
My soul cries for help, and my heart aches in disgust.
Sometimes reality is a bit obstructed, a bit obscure,
Navigating with no new destination but the previous,
Embarking on a journey to a once-familiar place
Where happiness lived, where love once lived—
In songs, a reminder that there was once a 'we'—you and me.
Love was simple.
Countless nights I've spent trying to find the warmth
And gentle feel of your arms when I lay.
Pillows we once shared I still have
With the sweet scent of your perfume still lingering.
Its calming effect misleads, and I imagine you here
Making music as you did with keys to my heart,
Hoping you know I still love you more than life itself
I find myself wanting to call, wanting to text as if—
But I can't. I was the one who hurt
To be then hurt by the absence of love,
The one and only love who woke every morning
With a bright smile, rain or shine, for I was your sunshine—

Proud to claim what gift you considered me, you cared and loved,
Giving more than enough. Such was your love.
And here I am attempting to erase history,
Start anew by suffocating the heart
Which still lives on the hope of your return.
A smiling face holds back what tears yearn to flood down my face
And wash what fake smile I paint for the world.
A constant search for that feeling—
The one I got the first time we met, and every time after that.
However, just as empty the search ends, leaving me wanting more.
Comparisons fall short and are anything but remnants of you,
And at every turn something becomes you.

Your heart is my home.
Your spirit my guide.
Your love, my inspiration.

Homeless

Awake, in yet another place
As unfamiliar as the last,
Carrying nothing but memories,
Having had to having lost
Your heart—I am homeless,
Missing your embrace,
Missing my space.
There, where I once was the only resident,
Now resides doubt,
Occupying all of my belongings,
All of your feelings
From your love to your attention.
I am homeless.
And, truth is, I miss my home—
There, where the music always played
And everything felt just right,
Never cold, always warm and tender,
Sheltered underneath your love,
Secured by everything you—
And all attempts to build again without you
Have been futile.
Every beautiful thought pains my soul,
Just as much as the memories I carry
And refuse to erase.

TONIO

Divorce

Married to a fantasy
With the ideals of a matrimony
Less than holy
Based on a lie,
Convinced you own me,
And I must abide and comply,
Becoming a recluse of sorts,
Homebound—under your surveillance,
Proclaiming a love I now know
Was nothing more than a sick obsession.
For I—who could not give of your expectation
But it is I—who now demands a divorce,
Wanting nothing more than freedom
From this imprisonment—
From you.

Home

Like a volcano it erupted,
Overflowing with love
At the sight of you,
Never in the past.
Never mind the past,
Never mind the rules of engagement
Living so long in the wild,
Forgetting it so
Recklessly endangering—
Taunting—flaunting—luring
Only to run and hide.
Untamed wanting captivity
Wanting a keeper,
But never anyone quite as astute as you
Unguardedly approaching the vicinity of my heart,
Fearless and ready to battle.
And so you won my heart,
Conquering uncharted territories,
Building something unfamiliar,
Laying the foundation
Of that which I now know as—
Home.

TONIO

After the Storm

The storm had passed, it seemed.
Minor aches and bruises, but alive,
I managed to save the only thing money couldn't replace.
And off I went, walking aimlessly through
What seemed like a wasteland.

Wasn't looking to find, nor be found.
In fact, I didn't want to be seen.
I was alone.
Everything I had I lost in a dreamland—
That paradise somewhere in the vicinity of love
But never quite the love.

I was angry.
'Why me?' I would ask.
'What if' and 'Maybe'—they were my worst advisors,
Kept me around long enough
Just to slap in my face
The truth I had always known.
Luckily, they, too, I lost in the storm.

Patience was running low,
Hope dwindling with every step,
Every corner I turned seemed dark.
There wasn't a sign of life,
Not a flower in sight,

But there you were—
Unannounced and uninvited,
Walking beside me
To a destination unknown.
And so I stopped
As you invited me in.

Hope didn't seem to live here,
Nor love.
There wasn't a welcoming smile,
Nor was there a sense of security.
But I saw the beauty.

I could hear you knocking,
Hesitant to answer.
I observed a while longer,
Refusing to let you in.
Slowly I begin to turn the knob,
Leaving the door ajar
As you did the same for me.

Attracted to your imperfections,
Faith in that I can restore any broken pieces,
Build up what fell,
I took that step in
Hand-in-hand, and
Together we smiled
As if to say,
'This is my home now.'

The Call

I was there once before,
Stuck between absence and presence
In a place infested with promises
More poisonous than the relationship itself
Where I lingered,
Awaiting endlessly for acceptance
To become. To be loved. To be yours.
But I was a friend, at best—
The one you didn't want to hurt,
The one you saw long ago
Worthy of taking home to Mom and Dad.
It was more than that.
I knew, and you figured I'd never know,
Since I always believed
You give and take without question,
But I knew. It was all another lie,
And my heart is on the line,
So I let go.
I untethered my heart.
From that place you'd put me
On the sideline
Awaiting a call I needed to make
With my life, my love,
And I did.
Only tonight you had the nerve
To attempt and

Take me back there
In the same way you did every time before,
Speaking enticing words,
Touching.
Only tonight I had someone waiting,
Someone who does in fact love me,
And I don't care that you now tell me
My absence is felt.

On the Other Side

Broken.

Barely beating,
Badly bruised,
Hardly any sign of life,
Walking without purpose
Alongside the street
Where victims of love go,
Where hopelessness is a religion of the masses.
Certainty—a past forgotten,
Love—an enemy to be feared,
To be avoided.
But you
Were on the other side,
A firm believer.
An enchanting storyteller
Erased and rewrote
A painful past, a beautiful present—
A promising future.
Face to face,
Hand in hand, lifted me up
Higher than the tallest mountain
To this place we now call heaven
Where fighting only brings us closer
And this thing we call love doesn't hurt—
It heals.

Blind Spot

Conditioned to believe it not,
A thing of here and now,
Always a thing of a distant future,
Or perhaps a lovely dream of dreamers
Who have yet to awake to a brutal reality
Of the nonexistent love
They so faithfully hold and hope for.
I was among them—
A devoted lover of romance
Always looking forward,
Never back or to either side of me,
Always missing; I thought—
Slowly losing hope,
And then suddenly
You appear in my blind spot
Out of nowhere with a delightful smile
And a powerful voice
Dangerously veering me off-course
And into a complete stop—
Crashing down all the walls of protection
Built solely out of fear,
Because now love is near.
Protection I no longer need,
For security you provide
With every reassuring look,
With every reason why me, instead.

And I believe you simply,
Because you arrived willfully and timely,
As in my dreams,
As here and now
In my beautiful reality.

Someone Like You

The pain of not having,
The pain of living without,
Silently torturing,
Slowly killing
The best of everything I had to give,
Losing strength,
Losing its way,
Misguided by lies and promises
You never meant to keep.
I know, because
You will never be strong enough to admit it.
And perhaps this is the end of a story
Meant to teach,
And the pain will only strengthen a once-weak heart
Easily misled,
Easily bruised.
But I still love you
More than you will ever know,
And the tears jerk me around
With every haunting thought
Of what will never be.
And so I surrender hopelessly—
Settling for what is given, not promised.
Hope is said to be the only relief,
And yet I fail in seeking it so,
Knowing I can't take back my heart,

TONIO

Not when it has settled
There where you are and where I wish to be,
And every attempt to forget ends in more pain,
Realizing someone like you
Is all we've known love to be.

Some dreams never die.
You're one of them,
Whether awake or asleep,
Always alive.
And I dream you here,
Close and very mine.
Time and distance both have yet to make me wonder,
Let alone stop dreaming of you,
My world of love.

Came across an old picture of you,
Thinking I was stronger now.
Attempted to feel indifferent
Testing my will.
Only I noticed in the reflection
A familiar symptom of love:
The undeniable smile
Exuding all the joy and happiness
I get from within—deep in my heart,
And I know—
Nothing's changed.
I'm still in love with you.

Someone who has loved truly and honestly
Will never apologize for having done so
Regardless of the outcome.

my kind of love

not a moment went by
Where I
Wasn't thinking of you.
Heck, I loved you,
I can admit with certainty,
Knowing truly there wasn't a thing
I couldn't do for you.
My morning glory—
My anticipation of all that is wonderful
And yet to be.
I was there for you
Regardless of how often it hurt
Not receiving.
I thought with time,
You will say more,
Give more—but that's not what happened,
Because while you're there
I'm here
In a place between is and was
Where I'm no longer hurting,
And where you're just now feeling my absence
Much too much late.
Much too much time has passed,
And I'm different now—
Wiser, even—
Understanding in all honesty

You were never the one for me,
Because, believe it or not,
Right here by my side is someone
Who's showing me all types of love,
But my favorite kind is the one
Where true love is never absent.

TONIO

The Secret in Your Eyes

Something's happening—
I don't quite understand it.
I'm afraid.
A sudden pause,
An unfamiliar feeling,
A beautiful thought
Of you, whom I just met—
And yet I feel I care,
Desiring more than just this moment.
Thinking beyond. Thinking forever.
Realizing beauty is all around me,
I brace myself.
Your smile is intense,
Radiating with love,
And I'm captivated in curiosity,
Amazed by how confident and freely
Your lips pronounce my name.
I'm enchanted.
Counting every second
Before each time your eyes blink
At exactly 7 seconds apart,
I keep looking,
Noticing the smallest details
That make your face so fascinating,
Tempting to kiss.
But I must wait:

There's a story underneath,
And you won't tell me,
But your eyes—they're willing to show
What your lips won't narrate
By the way they look at me.
I look back intently,
Ready to see.
I inch closer, and there
I see the shape of my heart in your cornea,
And right then I knew
You were more than a romantic interest.
You were, in fact, the one.

Sitting

Perhaps it's the thought of you I'm missing,
Or the empty passenger seat
I now stare at
Taking me on a ride
Through every moment from start to finish
Of when I thought we were
The best of what this world offered:
Unfiltered romance,
Belonging without titles,
Loving effortlessly and without speaking.
We just knew.
We just understood.
But sitting here, all alone,
I'm left wondering
How idiotic,
How foolish,
Having had nothing then,
Thinking so,
Firmly believing,
Quickly dismissing—
Now quickly realizing
You were all but a dream.

Thinking of You

I'm thinking of you
Every moment now,
Knowing surely I want you
For all that we can become,
For all that you are
Nevertheless,
Always the best,
Never wondering if
When we are—when we will.
Certainty is key,
Your smile is hopeful,
And your actions thoughtful.
I'll care because you're mine.

TONIO

Wreck

I'm a car wreck of emotions right now,
My heart beating so fast
Like the flashing of the hazard lights,
Only its dark inside my heart.
Panicking. Trying to eject this love.
The only love I've ever known.
A total loss of my time
Resulting in shattered dreams,
Broken promises, all of which
Now lay on the ground with the once-luminous
Guiding light
Who lit the darkest confines of my soul on fire.
But I cannot, with words, say goodbye
In this battle for survival
From a million words
Stuck between my mind and heart.
I want to survive.
I want to love again.
So I try and suffocate this love from within,
And yet it lives—it breathes—it loves
While I'm left with the painful injury
Of a broken heart.

Someday soon,
If not already,
I'll meet you somewhere else
Other than in my dreams.

nightmare

I thought, and that was my mistake.
Truth is, I have nothing,
Not with you,
Not now, not ever.
I simply
Endangered my heart,
Throwing it carelessly
Into a vicious cycle of lies,
Mauled by fear,
Eaten by doubts
That never seemed to dissolve
Into anything but more doubts,
And I—
Helplessly tried to escape
From the very same place
I thought to be safe
While you watched silently
As I was torn to pieces,
Becoming nothing of
He who was the embodiment of love—
And then I realized it was all a dream.
I can wake up
And fight back.

No Longer Us

A deafening silence
Between us,
Neither one courageous enough to ask.
And I won't speak
While it still hurts,
Prepared to walk away at once,
Too late to fix what's shattered,
And truthfully
A painful distance now exists
After so many years—
A brutal reality
Living in nothingness
From love to indifference.
You and I
No longer us—
Thus a separate entity.

Heart in Exclusion

Bounded by titles,
Governed by relationship ideals,
Neither one of us understands.
That is now my reality,
Lying beside you
Wide awake,
Feeling so alone,
Planning an escape,
Knowing I belong elsewhere,
Wishing I were elsewhere.
There is no love between us.
Perhaps there never was—
But all a fleeting desire,
Now a dire cry for freedom
From a heart suffocating in exclusion.

Transcendent Love

Perhaps by now you know,
And maybe you can't quite understand it.
That's okay.
I don't sometimes,
But love is that way—
Incomprehensible, yet undeniable.
I know, because I've tried
Running and hiding,
Only to find you again and again
With every turn and every step.
It's scary to think of losing you—
Imagining another—impossible.
Transcendent is our love,
Energetic in nature,
Soulfully enchanting,
Existing in a world far less superficial,
Far more divine in that—we didn't choose.
Instead, we accepted our hearts' desire
To unite.
To love.

To Love Yet Again

I prayed too long for your acknowledgment.
I cried too much for your love.
I wasted much of my time wondering
When I could have been loving.
I know, because I'm the one
Sitting here in solitude,
Watching all the lovers pass me by,
Flaunting what I dismissed,
Cherishing what I refused,
All for a dream I was in,
All alone.
I suppose I forgot everything I knew
About love, its habits and nature,
Arriving willfully and freely,
Healing instead of hurting.
Or perhaps you didn't care enough to wake me.
And now, here I am,
Well taught—badly beaten,
Bruised but unbroken,
Ready for love.

Love Stage

Sometimes I wonder
If I was too abrupt
In how I exited the love scene
Feeling like a play.
Perhaps it was fear
Or my obsession with perfection.
But I miss those memories
We created then—
You and I on that stage
On a weekend in Boston,
Acting as if love had once again come.
Never mind the backstory.

Your Hands

Your hands
Gently felt their way into my heart,
Crawling down every wall
And into the deepest confines of my soul,
Unlocking its doors,
Touching me in ways I'd never imagine,
Awakening my inner beauty,
Releasing love.

For the Brave Heart

Love isn't for the fearful
Nor faint of heart.
It's for the wild.
The reckless.
Requiring audacity and curiosity.
Willingness is futile
If you're cautious and abiding.
Spontaneity and activity
Are everything.
Naturally love
Is romantic in gestures,
Kind in words,
Unpredictable. Unplanned.
It satisfies abundantly
Your every desire,
Validating your existence,
Pampering your spirit
With a simple touch of serenity.
Suddenly you're speaking dulcetly
In a language
Of the divine.
Respectful. Purposeful.
Love is neither fiction
Nor fairytale.
It's factual. It's earthly.
It's beyond, but requires bravery.

TONIO

Romantic spirits,
You and I,
In human form
From city to city
Near and far,
Effortlessly enchanting,
Profoundly enamored.

Future

So I'm sitting here,
Thinking, wondering, imagining
My future—
It is more beautiful than a summer day,
More warm than a spring afternoon,
And, best of all,
It smiles brightly back at me.
It knows I'm here, and I'm real.

Sometimes I think myself crazy
Wanting this future. I call you; now—
More than a chance at tomorrow,
Because, for the first time,
I believe in something.
I believe in someone.
And there isn't a doubt.

You know it is real
When there isn't an impossible,
And possibilities are
Every time I look into your eyes,
Every time I hold a picture of you,
Feeling my heart jump at you.

With pain comes growth,
I keep saying—
Hoping at some point I'll believe it,
Fighting painful thoughts,
Knowing now for sure—
Nothing mattered.
You never cared.

Because Falling Out Hurts, Too

It's like walking on a treadmill,
Only I'm going downhill,
Holding on to everything,
Hoping it's strong enough,
Real enough
To withstand this betrayal.
But everything leads to nothing,
Walking infinite miles to nowhere,
Fearful of rock-bottom,
Afraid of the uncertain,
Pausing for a moment—
Not a second longer—
Every time the thought of you hits hard
Like rocks falling from the mountaintop,
And I'm left hanging,
Wishing I hadn't climbed so high up,
Only to fall out of love.

Incomplete

Senseless.
Loveless.
That was the sex
Erupting desires for more than
Casual encounters
In hopes of filling—
Only they empty the soul further
Angrily in disgust.
I must run.
I must soak in attempts to clean
And purify once again.
But I can't. I'm still thinking,
Wishing it was love,
Wanting a joyful smile
With kisses delivering special messages.
Only I'm left,
Incomplete.

if only for a single moment I could forget,
Pretend as if I did not know,
Perhaps then you can convince me.
But that which you did
I can never forget.

Love at First Sight

I remember the first time I saw you,
Thinking, 'Wow,
My God—'
And smiling simultaneously,
Feeling somewhat strange,
Immersed in the thought of yet a stranger
Whom I now know as love.

Love Ever After

Perhaps I am to blame,
But I wonder who, in fact,
Cares enough to interact
With the part of me I've hidden.
Most people will never understand
Love doesn't live on the surface—
Instead, in the depth of the human soul.
Admission into this enchanting place
Is neither easy
Nor free of obstacles,
But worth it all.
And once you're in—
There is no exiting
Love ever after.

Something Certain

The love of my life
I met on a beautiful night
Under a full moon
On May 5, 2012.
Ever since then
I've not been the same.
It was the first time my heart danced in excitement,
The first time I was floored,
The first time I felt alive—
But, as romantic as this all sounds,
We're not together.
We're not physically in a relationship—
At least not yet.
But something else remained.
Something grand.
Something certain.

In the Land of Broken Hearts

Just yesterday I was feeling alive,
Joyful and triumphant,
Involved and in love,
In a healthy relationship—I thought—
Feeding off love.
But I was mistaken, misled.

And waking up now
I took a closer look,
Only to realize it was poisonous
What you gave, what you fed.
So here I am now
In the land of broken hearts,
Aimless and loveless,
Almost dead,
Disgusted by the thought
Of how much I loved you,
Finding fault in myself
For having lost sight,
For not taking precautions.
But the craving was more powerful
Than my hunger for love,
So I indulged incessantly
Without questioning

TONIO

What I was ingesting.
So here I am without—
Among others who
Loathe and dishonor love,
Wallowing in the depressive nature of this land,
Convinced love is evil, love is poisonous.

But while they mourn in silence,
There is solace in my heart.
It beats ferociously still,
So I know I'll love again.

You're the best
Of my everything
In this world.
I love you.

no Fairytale

All alone on the side of the road,
Feeling abandoned,
Afraid and confused,
Watching all the happy faces pass by,
Wondering, 'Why not me?'
While I'm stuck helplessly,
Awaiting your rescue,
Frantically looking back,
Hoping I'd see you.
But this is no fairytale,
And you're no happy ending.
Can't fix what's broken,
So I'll push forward what's left of me,
Hoping someone can salvage this wreck.

I'm in love with you
Beyond words,
Beyond explanations,
Beyond reasons.
I cannot say that I'm afraid—
I'm feeling rather courageous,
Though love is dangerous.

Inside My Heart

You were there.
Inside.
Deeply rooted
In everything I believed love to be,
Pulling on every string
So much it hurt,
So much it destroyed
The only dream I've ever had.
And still I loved, knowing
You didn't deserve my heart.

Hopelessness

I'm surprised I'm awake—
Falling asleep—on empty,
Convinced I'd die
Aching with no remedy,
My heart—silent.
Paralyzed from the shock.
But I awoke—only I'm colorblind.
All I see is gray all around me
While hopelessness is reaching out,
Wanting to accompany my broken heart.

my Heart

It palpitates,
Never hesitates.
At your command,
It accelerates.
You own my heart.

Life and Love

We've been fooled and abused,
Emotionally obstructed,
Mentally instilled with beliefs
Of what brings falsehood into our hearts,
Money into their pockets.
We have a tendency to add value
To only what we deem aesthetically beautiful,
Except, our perception of beauty
Is skewed.
Life is the only true beauty,
Followed by the magical nature of love,
Which enhances life's beauty.

My Place of Choice

It's beautiful here
In your heart,
My place of choice,
Where the warmth of your love is everlasting
And I'm more than just a guest.
No need to second-guess.
It's something more than extraordinary,
Difficult to explain,
But here where I live
Is peacefully wild,
Securely locked,
And I am the only.

Love has a tendency
To beautify and rectify.
It isn't obedient,
Nor complacent.
It's combative,
It's revolutionary,
It's transparent,
Bearing unimaginable strength,
Capable of change,
Available to all who never defy
Nor doubt its existence.

Soulfully Romantic

My baby, you,
Significant and true.
More than enough—
Sufficient.
Incredibly beautiful,
Extraordinarily amazing.
I awake in your presence,
Feeling so divine,
So fine.
You're loving feels unreal,
Though it's real,
Missing you
Is every moment
I'm without.
No doubt
I can't promise
What's already been destined,
But I'll surely love you
Regardless.
You stole a piece of me,
And now I'm gladly yours.
Thanking you is never ending,
For my grateful heart admires you.
He adores you,
Finding a reason more each day,

Because you did it, baby—
You kissed my soul with your smile,
And that's how I know.
That's how love is discovered.

i Believe

Suddenly pensive
In a state of confusion,
Fooled by the only love I've ever known,
My heart unfamiliar and defiant,
Blind as ever. Rather useless.
Continuously yearning
For someone unworthy.
Refusing to see
Opportunities for something real,
Something worth beating for,
While my soul cries,
Tries to reach out,
But I'm just as weak. Just as stubborn.
Falling for every word. Every smile.
Until tomorrow,
When once again you play
The same song. Different verse.
Familiar yet different. Effective.
Because I believe,
Despite the truth.
Every time.

Dysfunctional Heart

I want to hate him—
My heart—
For disgracefully
Deceiving me,
Setting me up
To lose,
Never minding my reasons:
'Love is a business—
Just follow.'
And so I did.
Thinking perhaps the heart knows best,
I surrendered,
Giving of myself freely and purely,
Just because
This was love he assured.
We mustn't run just yet.
Love isn't perfect,
But logically it shouldn't devalue
Nor reduce.
And that's what happened
Every moment of every day
My soul cried freedom
While lying in a bed of lies,
Hugged by a stranger
Sleeping beside the enemy,
Hoping it was all a dream.

But no. It was real, and messed up—
Following a dysfunctional heart
Selfishly entitled
Racing to feed his hunger for real love
Who lied, boasting a strength he never had,
Masking the pain of yesterday,
Making believe it was all forgotten,
Only it never healed from the last accident.
The last bruise.
The last damage.

Passionless

I've been down this road before,
Long enough to know
Where and when it ends.
A promising beginning
Doesn't always equal a happy ending.
I know you mean well.
The intent is there,
And so is the willingness,
But the passion—that is missing,
And without it you cannot awake love—
At least not in my heart.
Real love is never ordinary,
And so I'll never settle.
It entices and excites,
It distracts and obstructs,
It alters
While creatively planning and anticipating
Our next time.
And I with you have yet to experience
Any of these symptoms of love.
But it isn't your fault,
And I'll never dare teach you

TONIO

How to love me,
How to romance me,
Or else I'll taint any purity
That still remains in my virgin heart,
Confusing and pushing it further from the truth
Of what is real,
Of what is love.

Afternoon Love

Just yesterday morning
I had been perfectly fine pretending,
Thinking I had enough, I had it all,
Smiling just long enough to amuse, to appease
The same people who cared just as much as I did
About nothing, really, but our egos
Promoting a superficial love of self,
Lasting just as long as the flash from the camera.
We so diligently work in our favor
Capturing our best side—our best features,
Forgetting our inside—our best qualities.
But here I was, sitting at a table full of people,
Feeling so alone, so unknown.
Never mind my sadness,
Because my emptiness hurt more.
All the supposedly enchanted admirers
Who promised love and support
I saw them no more,
I knew them no more
And, sadly but truly,
They never knew me.
Feeling hopeless, I'd turn my face away
Only to see you—there—
Sitting and smiling confidently,
Exuding self-love
That isn't loud

But silent and powerful—noticeable.
I saw that—I saw more.
With every glance I'd feel my heart
Revving up with excitement,
Suddenly energizing my spirit,
Refueling my hope for love—
Desiring what is real—
And that cloud of doubt would soon be lifted
The moment you looked my way,
Smiling—as if you knew all along
This afternoon would end with us
Discovering love.

A Moment to Remember

'Twas on a night like tonight
When my eyes and heart
Smiled simultaneously for the first time,
Falling for more than beauty,
Existing solely in a moment
Far and away from what fear I had,
Losing control, letting go,
And then silence.
This thing—
Love as I'd come to know it,
Suddenly real,
Suddenly settling in uncharted territory,
A place perhaps once reserved,
Now occupied.
My heart—
Finally speaking, finally agreeing
Encouraged a kiss I would soon never forget
And live a moment worth remembering.

Long Distance Pursuit

Sometimes the miles
Can scare an unsettling heart
Despite the beautiful smiles
And the unique qualities—
Instant gratification.
Forget patience.
'Life is short,' they say.
Never mind; divine time.
I can't wait.
Always a sign of caution,
For every strong heart knows
When it is, it will—

Now an Angel

We are so many
Gathered with broken hearts
Who love and miss you terribly,
Crying because it hurts non-stop,
Crying because your presence is needed.
We mourn your absence,
Even though we know
You're watching.

You left so suddenly
Without a hug or goodbye,
And we're left to wonder
If you knew how much we cared.
My soul aches
With every thought of you
While my heart,
Still paralyzed
From the moment I heard,
Tries to make sense
Of your departure
Much too soon,
Much too unreal,
Because we want more of you,
More of what made us
Love you unconditionally:
Your golden smile
Lighting up every spirit,

Your ability to befriend and conquer
Hearts of strangers—
And now the heavens.
We can't understand
Why you—why now?
But we'll trust God's choice in you
To guide and protect us all, or
Perhaps he needed more angels,
And now you're one of them.

The Outlier

I have yet to find that familiar feeling
Of yesterday,
Frantically searching—
Tempted to revisit memories
I thought were buried deep,
Only they seem to resurface
With every sound from my aching heart,
While down my face
The warm tears roll silently.
Why is no longer the question,
But when—if just yesterday
You were my everything,
Falling in love every time you were near,
Giving without a single doubt or hesitation,
All for that smile that just always touched my heart
In ways I could never explain.
I can't help but feel the painful thoughts
That now follow my every turn
As I continue to walk aimlessly away,
Only to end back where I started:
In the vicinity of your heart—but never in.

Thank You

I know better now.
Today I understand the why,
And it's because of you.
Yesterday, that was you—
Simply an experience,
A life's lesson,
One of which I learned from what you taught,
One of which brought me here,
A place where there is no wondering,
Where there is no doubt
Or fear to speak of love
Let alone live it.
I won't call you a mistake,
Because my feelings were true,
My love was real—
You weren't.
But none of that matters anymore,
And I thank you,
Because now I love me before anyone else,
And that special place I once reserved for you
Is now taken—
Yes, taken by love,
The kind that accepts and understands,

The kind that isn't afraid to show itself
Or give freely without having to hide—
The kind that isn't busy for me, for us.

If I were stupid enough,
I'd believe it so.
I'd be there still,
Disregarding your lack of commitment,
Your inability to risk winning Love,
Finding fault in everyone else but yourself.
For if it isn't like so,
Then it can't be so—
But I was aware,
Knowledgeable enough
To know that 'if' is a condition
Plagued by ambiguity
Neither here nor there.
You'll love me, so you said,
But only if—
And we'll be something more,
Only if—
And I was to conform to your uncertainties
And adapt to your conditions in order for—
Somehow it felt as though
I was the only one needing,
The only one willing,
Because it was always more about you than me,
And I allowed sacrifice and risk in the name of love,

Giving all and everything—without if's,
And in return the only way you could grow to love me
Was if—I—
And so I stopped you, because
My love is sacred, to be venerated—
My love—is forever. A definite. Never a maybe,
Loving me is a sure thing
To never be clouded with doubts
Nor based on conditions of convenience to you.
My love is unconditional as love is.

i Awoke

You should know there was a time
When I loved you more than anything in the world,
But not now, not anymore.
I—awoke,
I—understand,
I—know.
Somehow I confused
Familiarity with love,
Availability with stability,
Receiving in return
Your inability to give,
Your inability to love.
When I expressed, you ran—like a child
Fearful of my conviction,
Fearful of—
My ever-so-spectacular way of making you feel
Emotions you never knew you could,
But I understood.
You should know I knew more than you thought I did—
So I tried to understand, to tolerate,
While becoming well acquainted with a virtue—
Patience, we call it—
But this morning I awoke,
Realizing a lot more than what I knew I deserved.

So I smiled at the thought—of you
Missing all the parts of me
You gave up to fear.

It hits me suddenly—
And then silence—
As I grapple to understand:
Why again
Am I so in love
With the same dream,
The same person,
The same love?
Why suddenly this craving for love,
This ferocious appetite for your heart?

Let Go

Let go, I said—
Not once—not twice—
But a million times now,
Knowingly abusing my dignity
Bruising my heart
With every bit of rejection
From a love I wasn't promised,
Finding myself on the side of the road,
Contemplating ways to escape
This dangerous love affair
Between a dream and my reality,
Losing everything to nothing.

The Answer

I fell in love the moment I saw you.
I knew something would change from then on—
Only I didn't know you'd become my life,
Finding beauty in every thought of you, big or small.
I am extraordinary, knowing you love me back.
Sometimes you may doubt it
Because I don't say it enough—
Heck, sometimes I don't even behave like love.
But the best thing about our love
Is that it isn't perfect.
We're not constantly pretending
Or basing it on the superficial,
But instead, on a friendship we knew to nurture—
A love we knew to always respect.
So yes, I love you.
This will never change.
The only thing changing is,
I keep falling more and more in love
Every time you call my name,
Every time you remind me of who I am
And why you chose to love me—
Every time I sleep,
Knowing your thoughts are with me—
Knowing amazing is what we are.

Your Smile

It wasn't simple.
It came with a reason.
It wasn't just any,
But 'the' Smile
Shining brilliantly with a purpose.
Yours, but very mine
From the very first time
Beautifully telling—
Hiding nothing,
Saying everything,
More than happy to see,
More than happy to finally meet.
As real as love,
Your eyes and mouth all moved in unison
With passion behind every blink,
And the lines on your forehead
Beautifully formed patterns of infinity,
Revealing the amazingly beautiful face
I would come to love—
Not broken, not bent,
Fully developed and ready to conquer my heart
Without doubt or hesitation.
It was neither contagious nor dangerous—
So then I smiled back with the same intent,
Knowing this was it.

Let me in

Give me a chance to give all that I am.
I miss you, and I love you more than I love me—
And this is unusual, considering before you
I loved nothing and no one more than myself.
Be mine as I am yours.
Say yes with a kiss.
Take my hand so I know its OK.
Love me now, and never leave me.
I don't want to cry another night,
Because it hurts when you're not here.
Take all that I am giving,
All that I am willing to be for you.
I want you.
I do—so badly.
I love how it feels when we hug.
I know you care, so just be here.
I want to live you—every bit of you—
In and out, all hours of the day.
I'm ready to explore your world.
Let me in.

Undeniably Yours

I must have missed something
In the process of loving.
Seems I'm losing.
Every day is a new struggle,
An attempt to escape.

I've tried many ways to kill,
Only to find it more alive than ever, and
Undeniably yours—

It began so beautifully, so innocently.
Quite honestly, no one could ever compare—
No one could fill my heart the way you could
The moment we first kissed,
The moment I became
Undeniably yours—
And the first time I became whole,
I understood the power of love.

Just yesterday I was your everything,
Understanding without saying,
Speaking without thinking,
Loving without trying.
That was us—

Today I am a friend who loves you more than—
And still there isn't a thing I wouldn't do for you,
Only I don't think you know it—
Or perhaps you just don't care.
The moments I cherish most
I am attempting to bury,
Along with an undying love,
An undeniable truth,
Undeniably yours—

Love

Love comes in all shapes and sizes
And sometimes a single moment.
It is beauty beyond the basics of what the eye can see.
It lives on longer than any desire
And transforms an ordinary being into the extraordinary.
Love understands the why and how.
It never questions nor doubts,
But it tolerates and accepts.
It gives all, but also takes all.
Love amazes.
Love penetrates and satisfies your soul.
Love is human.
Love is sacred.
Love is scary when you're too weak to accept it,
Too much of a coward to live it,
To show it.
Love is what you lack when you don't care.
Love is the smile on your face.
It is the sound of your voice,
And the comfort you bring.
Love is your presence.
Love is your friend.

How I met you

I've never quite told you the story of how we met.
I smile every time I think about it,
Clearly remembering every detail of every moment.
This particular day began just like any other,
Only I'd meet someone like no other.
Somehow the moment I saw your face
It seemed familiar and dreamlike,
Only this time you had voice—and a special touch.
We smiled uncontrollably until the muscles in our faces got tired.
Neither of us seemed to care—
Strength was something we had plenty of, now that we united.
Questions we refrained from asking,
As everything made sense right there, right then.
Gone were the fears of heartbreak,
For we knew this was it—the promise, the life, the love,
And, more than the physical, we had a soulful attraction.
You hurt me every time you doubt my words.
You hurt me every time you wonder where my heart is,
And ultimately my love for you,
Which quite honestly has been the only honest thing in my life,
My only hope for survival, my only ambition.
I've grown. I've learned
Everything I am now
And all that is good and true I owe to you—to this love.
And yet you fail to see that nothing compares to the moments
When we simply sit side by side

Or when I gently poke here and there
As you giggle uncontrollably.
Need I remind you of the times when we hold hands?
More than a lovely gesture—
It's a sense of security, a sign of belonging.

Perhaps you can't tell, but I fall more and more in love with you
Every time we fight, because every time I've learned
Something new about you.
I wish you'd look far beyond what you don't think is...
In order to see that my heart is with you,
In the safest place I could find; your hand.

Passenger Side

Can't help but feel uneasy
Imagining someone else
On the passenger side
Where you belong
At my side,
But there is—
There's a stranger sitting here beside me,
Hopeful for something I know I can't give
While still pretending I'm whole
When everything is still with you.

The Poem

Like life,
You're a never-ending poem
Rhyming with reason at times,
And other times not,
But I suppose love is this way—
Nonsensical,
Yet all the more beautiful.

Wednesday Afternoons

i still remember Wednesday afternoons.
Always quarter past five
You'd visit with a cup a coffee,
Sometimes empty-handed,
But then you'd gift a kiss.
That was your thing,
And I grew to love and expect it.
Only I never had my thing for you,
Never bothered to try,
And last Wednesday I waited,
But you never came.

The Voice of Silence

A sudden faint echo
Replaying a voice still painful to hear—
Silence everywhere
In my mind and my heart,
A disparaging discomfort
Beating me down to my knees,
Cowering with fears,
Wallowing in tears.

Captured

It happened so suddenly,
In a moment's time
I'd lose it all.
That unassuming stranger
I'd just met—would soon become a thieving
Snatcher—taking without asking,
Giving without permission,
Unaware—I thought it safe to flaunt
In a heartless world—with no demand.
I thought it safe to wear on my sleeve
Just this one time—but your smile
Would quickly threaten my loveless existence,
Creating wants—creating needs,
And then I'd crave this ancient food—
They claim to feed the soul,
Make it soar up high to unimaginable heights,
But, fearful, I would run,
Only to be caught and greeted with love's name
And capturing my heart with a smile.

Dementia

Funny how suddenly you forgot
Years of love and sacrifice
That never sufficed.
And I did, at one point,
Begin to feel inadequate—
Quite unlikely of me, to be honest.
But it happened,
And it wasn't a good feeling
Questioning my sanity,
Thinking myself crazy—
When in actuality
I was just in a ruthless game,
Chasing perception,
Because none of what I thought we had was in fact.

The Kiss

He had forgotten how to smile.
He had forgotten what it felt like to be touched.
Hope, his only companion,
Had embarked on a journey to the other side.
Nights of endless dreams of you, so real—
They hurt when he awakes to the world without you.
'Why must I be so stubborn?
Why must I be so cautious
When every other heart seems wild and carefree?' he asks.

And then, along came you.
Followed by a beautiful evening
Under one full moon
I watched as you gazed into my eyes,
Then leaned to caress my face—
The face the world sees but does not know
As hidden behind every countenance,
A complicated story of me, the being.
Somehow you read every story and smiled.
I smiled, because finally someone understood.
Hand-in-hand we held each other
Ever so gently with our bodies clasped,
And slowly, around and around,
We danced to the beat of our hearts.
Oh my, have we never heard
Such sweet melodies of loving hearts!

Caught in this enchanting moment,
Our lips touched for the first time.
In this ultimate connection by our lips,
We then held on like glue to never let go.
I held you as you were now mine and I yours.
With my eyes closed,
I could see all the wonders of this world.
Without speaking,
I heard words my ears had never heard—
Untold stories of our journey to one another,
Promises of forever and promises of love,
All told in one kiss—The Kiss.

Suddenly all the feelings of lust, passion and love
Which are all masked in this one act
Were now clearly differentiated
As a tear of joy rolled down your cheek, and then mine.
Flowing freely as we now were, they fell into our lips.

Carefully listening to and processing every word,
He began to smile as he heard words we've never heard.
With my very own eyes
I saw beauty my eyes had never seen—
And, although blind,
He could sense beauty in your touch.
And he smiled yet again, for love had come.

Heart-burn

I am envious of broken hearts
Able to be fixed—
Mended—mind you,
While mine just burns incessantly.
Fueled by unpleasant thoughts of you,
It incinerates further,
Ravaged beyond recognition,
Rendered useless.

My Eyes

My eyes—
They've cried many nights.
Trickled with tears,
Tricked by fear,
Heavy with pain,
They've seen most of what was unimaginable.
Through darkness and grief,
They've maintained the light.
And I'm here now
On new grounds.
I'm here still,
And they smile with every glance at you.

New Song

I found a new song
While searching through an old playlist,
A place I never thought to look.
But there it was—
There you were—
And perhaps I never cared to listen further
Because of the title.
Judging by the genre,
I skipped over you—
Or I suppose you were too slow to start,
Inspiring no excitement at first.
And yet, here I am,
Dancing to the rhythm of your love,
Feeling so alive,
A sudden favorite
Stuck on repeat,
Playing my heartstrings like a guitar,
Sounding so beautifully harmonic—
How ironic?

Like New York City,

Love never sleeps.

Missing You

Missing you is an experience,
Sometimes beautiful,
Other times painful,
And the fear of losing
Is at times crippling,
But in the end
Our love is simply delightful.

Obsession

This shit has got me messed up—
The way I love you
And can't have you.
I can't hate you,
Because you've done nothing
But be honest.
"I get it, I understand," I keep saying,
Hoping I'll believe it,
But the more you reject me,
The more I want you,
And I keep
Diving deeper
Into this darkness
Of obsession.

Burdened

Somehow I keep finding myself on the floor,
Unable to bear the weight of your absence,
Watching it all bring me down,
Too weak to withstand,
Too broken to stand.
This is what I've become—
A sad, soulless figure
Struggling to find a reason
For why you're gone.

'Pawn'

Lately, we're all doing it—
Perhaps out of desperation
Or the lack of self-worth,
But we're pawning our hearts and souls,
Placing them in the hands and care of brokers
Looking to profit, looking to gain,
And again—we're all accepting it,
Getting in return less of what's owed,
Less of what we're worth.
It's no wonder we keep buying the lies
And exchanging our hearts and souls
For something temporary—
For a love, ordinary.

TONIO

'We Don't Talk Anymore'

Perhaps we said it all too soon,
Or our love is muted by something unknown
For which I still can't find a name,
And it makes no sense.
I mean, I couldn't get you to shut up before.
We always talked,
Sometimes all night,
Or even if, for a quick second,
We said everything with "I love you."
But now it's different, no doubt about it.
Our conversations are less and less,
Reduced to texts
So impersonal,
And I can't help but take it personal
Watching our love suffer,
Because we don't talk anymore,
And I just wish I could hear
What your heart is thinking like before,
And it doesn't speak to me.
You don't speak to me.

Tonight

Tonight I just want to dream
That all is well,
All is perfectly in place,
And you're right here beside me,
Where nothing's missing,
Nothing hurts.

my story

This is my story
About a time when I loved immorally
Such that I victimized my soul
Into paralysis,
And I became something undesirable,
Favoring abuse,
Feeling nothing,
Allowing you to hurt me
In ways I never imagined
A person can be hurt,
Where I would bathe in self-loathing,
Watching you pour more hate onto me
As I boiled with desire
For more dishonesty.
I wanted you to lie
More and more,
So I could pretend it was real
And you were really mine
And those friends really were just friends
And the hell I was living in
Was in fact a perfect example
Of a happy marriage.
A happy home.

Lies

I lie about you,
I lie about us
And the fact that we ever happened.
I guess I'm just too embarrassed
Of how foolish I was.

TONIO

Pretense

Fuck it!
There's nothing beautiful about this pain I'm feeling.
And I can't continue pretending it doesn't hurt.
I hate feeling so bitter
When I should know better.
It's not worth it.
You've changed me in undesirable ways,
Toiling with my emotions,
Playing with my love.
It's so hard to make poetic this feeling of uncertainty,
Watching you lie your way deeper into my heart,
Consuming my integrity...

For many, 'I love you' is freedom.
For me, it's a chain of words you throw at me
To keep me from leaving.

Wounded

j just wish it didn't hurt anymore.
I've nursed this wound—best I can,
Dressing it with forgiveness—
Sought remedy in forgetfulness—
And yet nothing.
The pain lingers.
You linger.

Amber

She's a promise,
Divine in every way.
I love her beyond reason
More and more.
I'm enchanted by her grace,
And every smile
Is yet another reason to continue.
Although she thinks it's temporary,
Our time—is set in forever,
And I'm keeping her
Like a promise.

Surrender

And the stupid part of me
Still wants one last fight
In hopes of winning back your heart,
Even though the war is over.

Heart-to-Heart

I'd never seen such sad beautiful eyes
Desperately crying out, "SOS!"
And I wanted to hug you tightly,
Knowing you'd been through so much.
And when I did,
I could feel the sound of your heart in distress
All the while hearing pieces of my heart shatter
As they hit the ground
Then I knew it was you.
It was love.

Revisiting You

Lately I've just been on a trip
Revisiting the past,
As if I hope to find newness
In what was once familiar,
And instead I keep stumbling
Upon nothingness.
And it's scary slipping
On familiar grounds
Where nothing is concrete
And you're at risk
Of drowning further and further...

Unread

You were my favorite story.
I loved reading you like a book—
Every word, every line, every page.
I couldn't put you down,
Reading over and over,
Rediscovering something new—
Questioning when I didn't understand—
So that I could.
That was love.
It seeks to comprehend.
But you never could pick me up to read,
And perhaps I wasn't interesting enough,
Or you just didn't care enough
To look past the beautiful cover art
And assumed that was enough
To judge my character,
Predict my story—
Leaving much of me unread.

Heartbreak

I'd be lying
If I said I wasn't trying
To forget you,
But the truth is
I can't.
Too much of you
Still lives in me,
And my heart fails
To open for anyone else
Who isn't the key bearer.

more to Love

I love you for reasons
You still don't understand,
And I want to show you
With every moment
That beyond your beautiful
There is yet more to love.

i miss you.

It's my ugly truth,

Considering how much pain you caused.

Hostage

Hopeless in search of love,
I was naive,
Immature
In how emotionally generous I could be.
You took that.
You took it all.
And supposing you loved me,
I became a willing victim,
Surrendering my heart into captivity
With your every word
While you kept me hostage,
Baiting my heart,
Feeding me lies,
Feeding me hope.
And I ate it all,
Trusting you were love
When in fact you were a ruthless thief of hearts
Looking for yet another conquest,
Yet another fool
To be at your disposal.

Leading Lady

I can't say that I know you,
Not anymore.
And perhaps I never did.
The person I loved
Was a lie,
A make-believe character you created
To play a role,
To play me.

nonsense

i can't help but feel this sadness
Overcoming my spirit,
Rooted from your absence.
And it's all nonsense to you,
Seeing you don't love me the same.
And while
I've accepted the pain,
Coping best I can,
I still pray that once again
You'll be mine.

Like the moon

The moon was a terrible witness,
A friendly light that night we first met,
That time we first promised.
But now I can't seem to find you,
Can't see your face
In a dark world without you.
And I'm walking on broken promises,
Chasing an evasive moonlight,
Hoping it would lead me back to you.
But I'm crazy to think so when,
Like the moon,
You, too, are avoiding me.

Staged Love

It's not always as perfect
As they make it seem.
Some relationships are staged
Like houses before you buy them,
Set to convey a certain ideal.
And it's sad that it has come to this,
Posing for the camera,
Anxious to post while faking a smile,
Awaiting praise and applause
From strangers who pry
When you cry.
And that's not love at all,
But merely a publicity stunt—
A hunger for attention and credence.
Because true love
Needs no validation from the outside
If, within you,
Both know with certainty
That it is real
And truly yours.

TONIO

Talented You

I know you always thought
I was the talented one,
But you're the one
With the real talent—
Having the ability
To make my heart smile
When no one else can.

Memories

And despite the months apart,
Nothing changed.
I still belonged to you.
I still wanted to be with you.
And I tried replacing old memories
With new ones,
Hoping they'd fade.
But they were enhanced
While I danced
To every new song,
Knowing you'd love them
Just as much.
But they always seemed
To miss a beat
While, bit by bit,
I crawled my way back
Into a past
That is always present and future,
That I will forever love.

Where it All Begins

You may not have someone special
Right now,
And that's okay.
But always keep the romance
Alive in your heart.
Keep the fiery passion burning,
Because self-love is ultimately
Where it all begins.

Denial

It's hard silencing the noise
While trying to sleep in denial,
Covered in questions,
Tossing and turning with doubts.
It's not just tonight—it's every night,
And I'm tired of pretending to be asleep
When you come home,
Because I can't face the truth:
I can't confront you.

Don't ever love with caution,

Or you're not loving at all.

Love's nature is wild and reckless.

FaceTime

i'll never forget the first time—
Our date on FaceTime,
Watching in amazement,
Repeating excitedly how beautiful,
How lucky it all felt—
This new beginning,
This, our time.
Surely promising in every aspect,
It was the closest I'd gotten to perfection,
Feeling so unbelievably enchanted in every way,
Ready to engage
And become something of another—
Something yours
And then nothing.
Somewhere along the way
We lost connection,
We lost each other.

Too Afraid

I guess I was wrong.
And one of us was too proud to say, "Stay."
Hence I am here, and you are there,
Somewhere away from the complexities of love,
Too afraid to multiply the memories.
And I figured you weak,
Lacking strength, and while
Supposing I'm wiser,
Having loved before,
I can't make you believe in something
You're too afraid to love,
Too afraid to lose.

Love Light

Your love adorned
The darkest ventricles of my heart
With lights of hope
Without which I can no longer see life.

Cruel Intentions

I left you there
On the side of uncertainty,
A road to nowhere,
Waiting anxiously for an answer,
Unfairly targeting your heart,
Victimizing your soul
In a prison of lies
While I fed you a mystery food
Tasting like hope,
Only it wasn't.
And it kept you alive
While killing your spirit.
And I didn't care.
I was already dead.

Scent of Love

You smell like love.
Divine and refreshing.
Exquisite in how you pamper my nose.
I adore the scent of confidence you exude.
The air of life I breathe.
You're the scent of love.

Waiting

Wondering if tomorrow will ever come,
You keep saying so,
And I keep waiting,
Wanting to belong to you.
But every tomorrow that's ever come
You've had time for everyone else but me,
But us—and I'm beginning to feel like a fool.

Silence is beautiful
When blanketed by love.

Desire

Missing you hurts.
Like hell, my heart burns
With the desire for your return.

Exit Wound

I just never thought you'd leave.
Like all horrific crime stories,
I thought it only happened on TV.
You were perfect—
More than I'd ever asked for.
And together we made amazing things happen.
I loved you blindly,
Neglecting all facts.
I didn't want to see the truth
Until it was too late,
And by then
You'd pierced your way into my heart
Like a bullet,
Lodging yourself deep inside,
Unable to be extracted so easily,
Unknowingly causing damage,
Violently puncturing my heart,
To then exit the way you did
Without a single notice,
Leaving a big mark.

TONIO

The Unknown

It's beautiful yet scary
Feeling yourself slip away
Into the unknown,
Gazing into your lover's eyes
For the first time.
I still remember
That fearful yet beautiful night,
Getting lost—to then be found
In a different realm,
A different world
Where it's all possible.
But more than that,
There was love.

murder

And sadly, it all ended tragically,
All too sudden, like an untimely death,
Leaving much unsaid—much unanswered.
And I'm barely hanging on
Like a widower in bereavement,
Grieving a love I adored—
A love you murdered.

Sometimes,

Depending on the severity,

A heartbreak,

It can maim you forever.

Taking Flight

in loving you
I've learned to fly
Without wings
And soar high
Above any cloud
Of doubt.

Dark Tint

You were just so special,
I could tell.
And not knowing your story,
I could still see the dark tint
Casing over your heart,
Hoping you'd continue
Going incognito,
Avoiding any passerby,
Avoiding the thief of hearts.
But I was in the neighborhood,
Looking to acquire,
Looking to love.
So I approached
Despite your darkness,
Took a quick look inside,
And there it was—
The heart of gold you'd been hiding
Behind shades of insecurities and hurt.

Rogue Heart

Destructive and unpredictable.
Dishonest and deceitful.
Such is this part of me—
Playful and loving one minute.
Vicious and disruptive another.
Conquering to then destroy,
Enticing to then evade
With no rules to follow,
No love to adhere.
Its vengeful nature is discerning,
Yet it makes me uneasy
Watching unassuming victims
Desperate for love,
Approaching the beast,
Not knowing the end will be unfavorable,
Not knowing my heart's gone rogue.

TONIO

Someday, Somewhere

Someday soon
You'll stop being just a dream,
And I'll have you next to me.
Somewhere away from here
We'll find comfort
In a distinct world of possibilities
Where love isn't make believe.

Survival

It wasn't fair what you did to my heart—
Drag it through a field of dreams
And then dump it in a minefield
As if love was the enemy.
But I survived—
Only to conquer real love.

Void

And everyday without you
Is numbing,
Feeling less of life
And more of this emptiness—
This nothingness that won't surrender
But surrounds me like love
When it was good.

There is absolutely no substitute

For real love.

Everything else is artificial

And really bad for you.

Kidnapped

You were astute
In how swiftly you kidnapped my heart,
Took it away to a place,
A paradise
Too beautiful to imagine,
Too perfect to ever want to leave you.

Racing

My heart is racing for you,
Hoping to win your love.

Strangers

It's upsetting to think
All the sleepless nights,
All the 'I love yous'
And promises
Had no significance,
Becoming yet again
Strangers in a loveless world
With much left unsaid,
Much left to desire.

Thief of Hearts

All I ever wanted was something real,
Someone who believed in love as much as I do,
To fight and to conquer anything.
And instead, I got you,
A thief of hearts
Amassing to satiate your ego.

Reality

Forced to cope
Without hope,
Lost in what feels
Like a bad dream.
Only it's real,
And you're no longer here...

Wishing

Just last night
I was thinking of you,
Wondering what it would feel like
Lying next to you,
Watching how you behave,
How you move.
I wondered it all,
But I wished more than anything
To be the one besides yourself,
To show you the kind of love
No fairytale can compare,
Where it isn't written or told,
But lived.

A Singular Moment in Time

Last night was amazing.
Experiencing the birth of a new love,
I watched hope come alive in your eyes,
Faith restored in my heart.
And, while smiling assuringly,
I kissed your lips for the first time,
Knowing for sure this was our time.

A Fine Line

An agonizing battle,
Having to love within boundaries,
Respecting the line
That is simply friendship
While loving more than.

What We Had

What we had
Was just a template of love—
Not quite the real thing.

Naked Heart

I hate the complacency in your voice,
Agreeing with everything for the sake of peace,
While I instigate yet another fight,
Hoping you'd disagree,
But it's useless.
And I want a fighter
Courageous enough
To make me uncomfortable
And still in love.
I want a monster
Who can scare the calm of complacency
And still evoke emotions yet unknown
While loving the ugly side of me.
Only I know, because
No one else has cared enough
To uncover my naked heart.

Being without you
Is the absolute absence of hope.

Harmony

There's something special
About falling asleep on your chest,
Feeling the warmth of your skin against my face,
Listening to an orchestra of heartbeats
Playing in one accord—
The sound of love.
The sound of life.

Band-Aid

Hurt and ashamed,
I faked a courage I didn't have,
Lied about being OK
When I wasn't.
When I'm not.
And I dragged you along,
Knowing you were good—
Too good.
But I was seeking a remedy,
Something to bear the burden,
Ease my pain,
Failing to face the problem,
Ignoring that this was more
Than a superficial cut.
I used you like a Band-Aid,
Hoping you'd cover up my wound,
Help me forget
Until I heal—
But no.
I'm still hurting.
The cut is still fresh,
Too deep to treat with ease,
And I'm still in love.
No matter how close you are,

How tightly you stick to me,
I am infected with anger and hate.
And you can't protect me from
This pain that consumes my soul,
Cowering every time
Thoughts of what was,
Throb me with insult.
I am weak.
I am deeply wounded.

'Good Morning'

I'm still not used to this new name
Texting me 'Good morning.'
I don't think I ever will.
Feels like winter still,
Despite it being peak of summer,
When you were my ray of sunshine.
And now I'm followed by cloudy days
Where nothing excites
And no one compares.

5 Star Hotel

I understood the world in which we live now,
Where everything comes at a high cost.
Business is ever growing,
And owning a home is almost impossible,
Considering all the maintenance
And the lack of patience thereof.
Sadly, the same change happened
With people and the way we love:
High egos, difficult to maintain,
Selfishness too severe to withstand any trials.
And I'm adjusting to the new norm of society
Whereby we rent and lease space,
And nothing is forever—
Temporary occupancy,
Temporary interest.
And I'm OK with change.
Such is life.
And so I converted my heart
Into a 5-star hotel
Where, no matter how long your stay,
Love is always genuine and qualitative,
A luxury in today's society
Of cheap and artificial love.

Everything you receive
Is personalized, never recycled,
Attentive and detailed
In how I operated this space.
It's no wonder you chose to stay a while,
Working hard to remain a guest,
Loving long enough to become
An owner of my heart.

Tethered

And I waited
In the vicinity of your heart,
Tethered to your uncertainty
While meandering hopelessly,
Wishing you'd soon set me free.
But I realized you liked me better this way,
And I needed to set myself free.

Peaceful Resolution

Some days I just want to reach out,
Say 'hi' like old times,
But I never do.
Getting lost in a million thoughts,
All very persuasive,
I return to the absence of you—
Discomforting, yet a peaceful resolution
To a time when I loved without sanity.

You are the only story
I can't seem to *finish*.

About the Author

Antonio (Tonio) Centeio was born in 1987 as the oldest of six children on the scenic island of Fogo, Cape Verde, off the west coast of Africa, where the picturesque landscape of fertile farmland, endemic plant gardens, and the volcanic mountain Pico do Fogo shaped his romantic view of the world at an early age.

At age seven he immigrated to the United States with his mother and two brothers for a better life, all the while writing stories and detailed expressions of his innermost thoughts and feelings. This turned him in a poetic direction, and he found himself feeling a profound sense of freedom and wholeness whenever he completed a new poem. This feeling, bolstered by the numerous positive reactions his posted poems received, convinced him that poetry was his natural outlet for his emotions. His near-death experience on March 11, 2015, coupled with encouragement from many friends and fans to pursue his poetic talent more fully, confirmed his calling as a poet and spawned his first book, *A Book About You: A Heart's Journey to Love.*

A resident of Dorchester, Massachusetts, Tonio is working on a novel to be released in 2017. He aims to write and publish Spanish soap operas and more poetry books in the future. When not working or writing poetry, he pursues love, romance, music, fitness, power-naps, friends, family, and life itself.

You can contact Tonio on Facebook (facebook.com/ iamtonio1987) and Instagram (iamtonio1987).

Made in the USA
Middletown, DE
18 August 2017